Bertha of the Big Foot
(Berte as grans piés)
A Thirteenth-Century Epic
by Adenet le Roi

MEDIEVAL AND RENAISSANCE
TEXTS AND STUDIES

VOLUME 417

Bertha of the Big Foot
(Berte as grans piés)
A Thirteenth-Century Epic by Adenet le Roi

Translated by
Anna Moore Morton

Tempe, Arizona
2013

THE ARIZONA CENTER FOR
MEDIEVAL &
RENAISSANCE
STUDIES

Published by ACMRS (Arizona Center for Medieval and Renaissance Studies)
Tempe, Arizona
© 2013 Arizona Board of Regents for Arizona State University.
All Rights Reserved.

Library of Congress Cataloging-in-Publication Data

Adenet, le Roi, active 13th century.
 [Berte aus grans piés. English]
 Bertha of the big foot (Berte as grans piés) : a thirteenth-century epic / by Adenet le Roi ; translated by Anna Moore Morton.
     pages cm. -- (Medieval and Renaissance texts and studies ; volume 417)
 "This volume is an English prose translation of the poem as edited by the pre-eminent Adenet scholar, Albert Henry" [Genève : Librairie Droz, 1982. Textes littéraires français ; v 305] -- Introduction.
 Includes bibliographical references.
 Summary: "The first translation of Adenet le Roi's Old French epic "Berte as grans piés" into a modern language. Includes an introduction and notes" -- Provided by publisher.
 ISBN 978-0-86698-465-2 (alk. paper)
 1. Berta, Queen, consort of Pepin, King of the Franks, 726-783--Romances. 2. Pepin, King of the Franks, -768--Romances. I. Morton, Anna Moore, translator. II. Henry, Albert, 1910-2002. III. Title.
 PQ1431.B2E5 2013
 841'.1--dc23

                                                            2013006302

∞
This book is made to last. It is set in Adobe Caslon Pro,
smyth-sewn and printed on acid-free paper to library specifications.
Printed in the United States of America.

TO

JERRY

Front Cover:
The miniature on the cover is from the beginning of Adenet's work *Cléomadès* in the manuscript collection ARS MS-3142 of the Arsenal library in Paris. According to Albert Henry,[1] it represents Adenet, standing to the left and wearing the crown of the king of minstrels, with Jean II of Brabant, Queen Marie of France and Blanche-Anne, her sister-in-law, who had recently returned from the court of Spain as a widow. Blanche-Anne is telling the story of *Cléomadès,* which she brought back from Spain. Marie of France was the daughter of Adenet's first patron, Henri III of Brabant. In the illuminated letter below the picture, Adenet is writing the story.

---

[1] Albert Henry, *Biographie d'Adenet; La Tradition manuscrite* (Geneva: Slatkine, 1996), 95–96.

TABLE OF CONTENTS

Acknowledgments	ix
Introduction	1
Select Bibliography	9
Bertha of the Big Foot	15
Notes	109

Acknowledgments

Without the encouragement and help of Paul Barrette, this translation would never have been written. He has read every word of it and made innumerable corrections and suggestions. Any remaining mistakes in this text are mine alone.

Introduction

Berte as grans piés is a poem written in Old French in the 1270s by Adenet le Roi, a poet from Brabant. This volume is an English prose translation of the poem as edited by the pre-eminent Adenet scholar, Albert Henry. Adenet's poem relates the betrayal of a Hungarian princess (the future mother of Charlemagne) who comes to Paris to marry the French king. At length those who betray her are found out and punished, and Berte (Bertha) is re-established in her rightful position, from which she had been removed.

Life of the Author

Although Adenet le Roi's exact birth and death dates are unknown, he gives information about himself in his works; and the records of one of his employers reveal more. He says he was taught to be a minstrel by the good Duke Henri III of Brabant, at whose court he apparently grew up. After the death of Henri, Adenet remained for a time with Henri's sons but by 1270 was a minstrel at the Flanders court of Gui de Dampierre, himself a poet. The counts of Flanders, though not of Brabant, were under the suzerainty of the king of France.[1] Although both Flemish and French were spoken in Brabant and Flanders, both Gui de Dampierre and his friend Duke Henri III of Brabant cultivated the French language (*Biographie*, 17–18). Gui traveled quite a bit, taking Adenet with him, notably on a year-long trip through France and Italy when they went down to the Mediterranean to join Louis IX (Saint Louis) for the Eighth Crusade. A few months after they reached the Mediterranean, Louis IX died of the plague during the siege of Tunis, and the crusade was disbanded. Gui and his entourage returned home through Italy.

Gui maintained close ties with the French court and French nobility (*Biographie*, 36). The largely Parisian French in which Adenet writes was probably nurtured by these contacts (*Biographie*, 43). Adenet tells us that he wrote his last work, *Cléomadès*, at the request of the French queen Marie, who was the daughter of his first patron, Henri III of Brabant. Adenet fashioned *Cléomadès* from a story told by Marie's sister-in-law, Blanche-Anne, daughter of Louis IX, who, widowed, had returned to France from Spain. Adenet sent Marie a copy of his

---

[1] Albert Henry, *Biographie d'Adenet* (Geneva: Slatkine, 1996), 36.

work *Les Enfances Ogier* as well. Adenet served Gui for thirty years (*Biographie*, 30), writing his four book-length poems (the one not yet mentioned is entitled *Buevon de Conmarchis*) between 1269 and 1285. His title *le roi* indicates that he was master of diversions, head of the other minstrels, and no doubt knew much literature and music. Gui de Dampierre fell out of favor with the French monarch, was twice imprisoned by him (*Biographie*, 47), and died in 1304. The last reference to Adenet in household records is in 1297.

Artistic and Thematic Aspects of the Poem

Berte was written as, and has been classified as, a *chanson de geste* or epic poem belonging to the *Cycle du Roi*, the group of Old French epic poems which relate to Charlemagne. The poem is written in *laisses*, the characteristic verse form of the *chansons de geste*. It features dramatic, violent conflict, and the fate of a nation is at stake in it. However, its lack of military battles, the women characters in its leading roles, and its emphasis on psychological portrayals persuade some critics that its genre is actually more *roman* than *chanson de geste*. Sarah Kay, however, takes issue with the idea that the presence of women in a *chanson de geste* adds a *roman* characteristic. She notes that the *Chanson de Roland* establishes for critics a model of the epic that features a community of males fighting for a societal ideal. Women in later epics have been perceived as distracting from this focus by introducing a concern for the individual, a trait of the *roman*. Yet Kay points out that women (often Saracen princesses) in Old French epics participate fully, even at times militarily, in the politics of society.[2] She rejects the idea that the mere addition of women to an epic poem adds a romance element and compromises the epic's concern with society (32). And, Kay observes, though most epics are full of violent conflict, several hardly include it (49). On the evidence of these two points, then, Kay would declare *Berte* a *chanson de geste*, and since it does not involve a journey of quest, a signal structure of the *roman* according to Kay (49), its exploration of individual sensibilities is its only salient characteristic left to liken it to the *roman*. The perspectives Sarah Kay provides on the Old French epic genre recall points made by William Calin in the conclusion of a study in which he explores the diversity of characteristics within the Old French epic. Calin reminds us that

> A literary genre is the totality of the individual works which make it up, not a rigid standard established centuries later in the academy; the medieval epic is no more pure or purposive than the modern novel or lyric. It is no more possible to determine which poet or novelist (or which traits of the *chanson de*

---

[2] Sarah Kay, *The Chansons de geste in the Age of Romance: Political Fictions* (Oxford: Clarendon Press, 1995), 29–38.

geste as a whole) should be considered the ideal than to determine which poet or novelist personifies absolute supremacy in more recent times.[3]

Adenet is an accomplished storyteller. The events in his narrative follow one another plausibly and smoothly; the characters are consistent; the dialogue seems natural. These are no mean accomplishments, and are perhaps particularly to be appreciated in a medieval author. With detailed comparisons, Régine Colliot shows the superiority of Adenet's version of Bertha's story to several earlier and later versions. Adenet reworked the story with distinct improvements in the logical succession of action and in the presentation of especially Bertha's character, giving her a nobility, dignity, and sensitivity lacking in other Berthas. Adenet excels in revealing Bertha's emotional life.[4]

Adenet also succeeds in giving with a few well-chosen details a sense of his characters' physical surroundings and a view of what occurs in them. An example of a justly treasured passage of his description is the panorama of Paris as seen by Blanchefleur from the heights of Montmartre (lines 1961–1972).

A remarkable and unusual aspect of Adenet's *Berte* is its versification. He wrote the poem in monorhyme *laisses* of alexandrines. Each *laisse* with a masculine rhyme is followed by a *laisse* with the rhyme in the feminine form. For example, a *laisse* with lines ending in *aine* would follow one with lines ending in *ain*. A few of the one hundred forty-four *laisses* stand alone without a corresponding masculine or feminine *laisse* to accompany them. Régine Colliot observes that these stand-alone *laisses* signal a change in the action (1: 168). Albert Henry remarks upon the variety of Adenet's rhymes, the absence of undue repetition of rhymes or wordiness—in short, the poet's skill in carrying out his chosen scheme and his improvement over his efforts with the same method of versification in *Buevon de Conmarchis*.[5] In a few cases, apparently the exigencies imposed by the rhyme scheme lead the poet to compose statements that may strike the reader as strange. For example, in line 847 he describes Bertha's complexion by saying, "Her color was not like an owl's." Again, in line 927 Bertha comments on her fear of being devoured by wild beasts by remarking, "They will sooner eat me raw than cooked." Although several other such examples could be cited, the natural ease and smoothness of Adenet's thousands of other lines in the poem offer much to admire.

The most distinguishing feature of *Berte as grans piés* is that the principal characters are women, a circumstance rather rare in medieval French literature,

---

[3] William C. Calin, *The Epic Quest: Studies in Four Old French Chansons de geste* (Baltimore: Johns Hopkins University Press, 1966), 246.

[4] Régine Colliot, *Adenet le Roi: "Berte aus grans piés": Etude littéraire générale*, 2 vols. (Paris: Picard, 1970), 2: 53–96.

[5] Adenet le Roi, *Berte as grans piés*, ed. Albert Henry (Geneva: Librarie Droz, 1982), 44–45.

especially in epics. Although medieval French literature does not lack for strong and important women, they usually share a large part of the story with men. Even in epics with eponymous heroines such as *Florence de Rome* (early thirteenth century), men determine and execute most of the action. Similarly, *Aye d'Avignon* (about 1200) is much less about Aye than about the men around her. In *Parise la duchesse* (second quarter of the thirteenth century), Parise, buffeted by misfortune, does less to advance the action than do the male characters. In *Berte,* however, the focus of the narrative is upon the women—and not one but several; they make the key decisions and take the crucial actions in the story. Male characters are relegated to minor roles. In addition, Adenet engages the reader's emotions with the women right away and gives each one a distinct personality. Immediately, our sympathies are aroused for Bertha by the portrayal of her grief at leaving her homeland and her family to go far away to marry a strange king. At her mother's final parting with her, she is so overcome with emotion that she faints. We participate, too, in her mother's sorrow, though she maintains a show of strength and encouragement for Bertha's sake. By the time Bertha is betrayed, we are well aware of her youth, innocence, and sweetness. Meanwhile, we witness the glee and zest with which her evil servants, another mother and daughter, plot to betray her. Later on, the dreams of Bertha's own mother prepare us for the intuition and the urgency of emotion that will lead her to uncover the plot against her daughter.

The managerial and leadership roles women assume in *Berte* also appear in two of Adenet's other works, *Buevon de Conmarchis* and *Les Enfances Ogier.* Though the entire focus in these poems is not upon the women, their importance to the action and their participation in it are highlighted and privileged. Gloriande in *Les Enfances Ogier* repeatedly extricates knights from difficulty, sees that truth and justice prevail in their affairs, and exercises compassion. In fact, Gloriande's intervention saves the honor of both the co-heroes in the story; and without her work, Ogier himself might not survive. In *Buevon de Conmarchis,* the warriors act out of their devotion to the matriarch Ermengart; they fight not to win her love but to honor it. Fervent and constant in her support, the heart and soul of her family of warriors, she directs their action through the force of her spirit. Even Clarmondine, the relatively inactive heroine of *Cléomadès,* manages to control her fate through the use of her wits. The women in *Berte* and those in Adenet's other three works who earn their narrators' approval are noble women and the worthy wife and daughters of the good Symon, who, although below the class of knight, serves the king in an outlying area and is prosperous. The villains in *Berte* happen to be servants, two women and one man, serfs whose freedom Blanchefleur had purchased. One is characterized as an "old woman." The reader may wonder if class of origin, age, and gender intensify the characters' and the narrator's rage against them; for frequently both characters and narrator express their anger by cursing these villains, almost always going so far as to invoke divine destruction upon them. Even the gentle Bertha utters such words a few times. The speech of all the characters is so permeated with references to God, declarations of devotion to him and of submission to his will that there can be no doubt of the deeply religious context of their lives. Therefore, the frequent occurrence of these calls for God's destruction of others, as much as they would appear at odds with Christian belief, seem to reveal that such sentiments were perfectly honorable and acceptable in the author's milieu. Perhaps the curses represent a transference of the battlefield idea that God means the Christian to destroy the infidel and will lend the warrior assistance in so doing. In this poem of 3,486 lines thirty-five curses appear, only two of which omit God's name (one substituting Mary's) and only six stopping short of wishing for the person's destruction (wishing instead for grief or a bad tomorrow). In *Buevon de Conmarchis*, probably Adenet's first work and comparable in length to *Berte*, expressions equivalent to "May God destroy you" are used eleven times, all but twice by the narrator, who applies it to Saracens. In *Les Enfances Ogier*, only two curses are spoken—both by the narrator, who asks God first to bring evil to, then to destroy, a villainous Saracen knight. No curses at all appear in Adenet's final work, *Cléomadès*. An examination of ten other illustrious works of twelfth- and thirteenth-century French literature reveals overall a sparing use of the curse in any form, an exception being Béroul's *Tristran*. However, five late twelfth- or early thirteenth-century epics scrutinized for curses contain more than do the ten works mentioned, though not as many as *Berte*, possibly indicating a tendency toward cursing traitors and other enemies rather freely in later epics. Nevertheless, the frequency and virulence of the cursing in *Berte* appears to be a somewhat unusual feature and may have to do with the class, gender and age of those cursed. (A note contains titles of works examined for curses.)

Sources and Influence

The popularity of Bertha's story attests to its importance in medieval literature: some twenty works of the Middle Ages retell it in several different European languages. Most of those were written after Adenet's. Two brief accounts in French, one in prose and the other in verse, predate Adenet's *Berte*; but his 3,486 line poem is believed to rework a version of which no trace remains. In the fifteenth century, a French prose version based on Adenet's *Berte* and entitled *Histoire de la Reine Berte et du Roy Pepin* appeared.

Henry lists various folklore motifs that occur in *Berte*, for example, that of the substituted bride, of the wife abandoned in the forest, of women gathered in the embroidery room, of an animal who leads to a lost person, of an encounter between a knight and a maiden (*Berte as grans piés*, 33). In volume one of her two-volume general literary study of *Berte aus grans piés*, Régine Colliot devotes a lengthy chapter to the examination of folklore motifs in *Berte*.

Although Albert Henry notes that the events in *Berte* have no counterpart in the Carolingian history they purport to represent, Bertha's betrayal and attempted murder do find historical echo in the accounts of Gregory of Tours of French and Spanish princesses in Merovingian times of the sixth century. These princesses, too, met with betrayal and violence. Gregory tells us that when King Sigibert sought a wife worthy of a king and married the Spanish princess Brunhild, King Chilperic, not to be outdone, promised to forsake the several wives he already had of servant class and asked for and obtained the hand of Brunhild's sister, Galswinth. The marriage aroused the jealousy of his former wife Fredegund, whose machinations finally resulted in Chilperic's ordering a slave to strangle Galswinth. She was found dead in her bed.[6] Later on, Chilperic and Fredegund's daughter Ragunth was betrothed to the Visigothic king. She was sent to Spain to marry him with many wagon-loads of treasure: silver, gold, fine apparel, and horses. Although an army escorted her, she was robbed steadily by people fleeing the entourage. When she paused at Toulouse to make repairs so as to present herself properly to her bridegroom, word came of the murder of her father. At that, a nearby chieftain confiscated her treasure. She was eventually robbed of all her possessions (128, 142–44, 150). Tribulation and misadventure may not have been uncommon for medieval women traveling afar to marry. Bertha's story may represent similar experiences of numerous other women.

Charlemagne's mother's name was actually Bertrade, not Berte; and she was French, not Hungarian; she was the daughter of the Count of Laon (Colliot, *Adenet*, 1: 34). However, Colliot informs us that good relations between the French and the Hungarians existed from the eleventh century and cites royal marriages between the two countries that took place in the twelfth century, notably that between Bela III of Hungary and Marguerite of France, daughter of Louis VII and his second wife, Constance of Castile (224). Furthermore, Hungarian students went to Paris to study (226). Colliot's sources reveal that the roads Adenet has his characters travel on were actually there. The old Roman roads had been maintained, and the twelfth and thirteenth centuries saw further work on the roads (232).

Charlemagne's actual mother, Bertrade, effected some important negotiations at the beginning of his reign. After the death of his father Pépin, Charles shared the throne with his brother Carloman. The duke of Bavaria and the king of the Lombards, Didier, sought to align themselves with Carloman against Charles in a civil war. However, Bertrade traveled to Lombardy and got an agreement for Didier's daughter to marry Charles and for Didier's son to marry Bertrade's daughter. The pope, fearing that an alliance between Charles and Didier would threaten papal lands, protested vigorously. Bertrade responded by persuading Didier to restore the papal lands that he had seized, which ended

---

[6] Gregory of Tours, *The Merovingians*, ed. and trans. Alexander Callender Murray, Readings in Medieval Civilization and Culture 10 (Peterborough, Ontario: Broadview Press, 2006), 58–59.

the pope's opposition to Charles's marriage. When Carloman died a year later, Charles repudiated his Lombard wife, no longer needing that alliance. Bertrade's diplomatic efforts, though not upheld, were crucial when they took place.[7]

Manuscripts, Editions, and Editorial Policy

Nine manuscripts exist of Adenet's *Berte as grans piés*. Designated as ABCDFGMR and w (a fragment), they are housed in libraries in Paris, Rouen, and Brussels. Scholars have found that five of them, ADGCR, are closely related; RF and w make up another group; M does not closely resemble any other. Manuscript A may have been copied before 1290; D, also late thirteenth century, was probably done in the same workshop. G was also prepared at the end of the thirteenth century. The other manuscripts date from the fourteenth century. The closely related five are judged the best; and within them A and D, which are very similar to one another, are the best, G also being very good (*Berte as grans piés*, 9–11). Albert Henry followed A and used D and G for cross-checking. The manuscripts were judged by their date, completeness, and consistency (*Biographie*, 196–227).

Editions of *Berte aus grans piés* were published by Paulin Paris in 1832, Auguste Scheler in 1874, Urban T. Holmes in 1946, and by Albert Henry in 1963 and 1982. Henry's 1963 edition was the fourth in a five-volume series of the four known works of Adenet entitled *Les Oeuvres d'Adenet le Roi*, published from 1951 to 1970. The 1982 edition was a re-publication of the 1963 edition in a Textes Littéraires Français format. Henry used the title *Berte aus grans piés* in the earlier edition but *Berte as grans piés* in the later one, where he explains in a note (175) that *as* is the more common preposition and that, although he had never considered that Manuscript A, which he chiefly followed, had a title, the phrase *Berte as grans piés* does appear in the explicit of Manuscript A. Manuscript B, he notes, has *aus grans piez*. Henry's edition is considered definitive, and Henry remains the foremost authority on Adenet's life. In his five-volume series on Adenet's works and in his introduction to *Berte as grans piés*, he provides information about Adenet's life in extensive and fascinating detail.

This translation, the first which translates Adenet's poem into English, renders the work into prose. In most instances, the translation has been line-for-line although occasionally words from one line are placed on the next line. Adenet's own style in this poem is simple, clear, and direct. He does not indulge in many verbal embellishments, depending perhaps on his elegant rhyme scheme to give his dramatic story poetic effect. The translation has therefore sought for clear, simple language and has aimed for as literal a translation as possible without resorting to unidiomatic English. The author makes extremely frequent use of

---

[7] Andrée Lehmann, *Le Rôle de la femme dans l'histoire de la France au moyen âge* (Paris: Editions Berger-Levrault, 1952), 118–19.

the intensive *molt*. The translation attempts to vary somewhat from *very* and *greatly* to reduce monotony. Certain adjectives (examples, *sage, debonaire, enseigné*) take on various nuances of meaning according to the situation. Their translations vary in consequence.

Adenet often switches between past and present tense for no apparent reason, sometimes in the same line or passage. Along with others, William Kibler points out that Old French writers did use the imperfect tense to indicate duration, repetition, and customary action and the preterite and present perfect for completed action. They also used the historical present to emphasize the immediacy or tension of a moment.[8] Although Adenet makes use of all these functions, Kibler's observation that in Old French texts "not all tense shifts are meaningful" (94) certainly applies to Adenet's *Berte*. The past tense has been maintained in this translation.

The author or scribe often varies the spelling of the names of the characters as, for example, in *Blancheflor/Blancheflour; Floire/Flore*. The choice of form of a character's name to use in the translation was made to retain a French flavor without jarring English orthographic sensibilities. *Blanchefleur*, a modern French form, is used; and *Pépin* is accented though no accent appears in the Old French. *Rainfrois* and *Heudris* have been allowed their final *s*'s on the examples of *Jacques* and *Charles*, but *Symon* and *Moran* have been written instead of *Symons* and *Morans*.

Adenet uses the plural *feet (piés)* in his title. However, I feel it best to stay with Bertha's traditional name in English, Bertha of the Big Foot. Like Bertha, the creature known in English as Big Foot has two big feet; but they are indicated, as are Bertha's by an expression in the singular.

---

[8] William W. Kibler, *An Introduction to Old French* (New York: The Modern Language Association of America, 1984), 93–95.

Select Bibliography

Primary Sources

Adenet le Roi. *Berte as grans piés*. Ed. Albert Henry. Geneva: Librairie Droz S. A., 1982.

———. *Berte aus grans piés*. Ed. Albert Henry. Paris: Presses Universitaires de France, 1963. Vol. 4 of *Les Oeuvres d'Adenet le Roi*. 5 vols. Paris: PUF, 1951–1971.

———. *Berte aus grans piés*. Ed. Urban T. Holmes, Jr. University of North Carolina Studies in the Romance Languages and Literatures 6. Chapel Hill: University of North Carolina Press, 1946.

———. *Buevon de Conmarchis*. Ed. Albert Henry. Bruges: Rijksuniversiteit Te Gent, 1953. Vol. 2 of *Les Oeuvres d'Adenet le Roi*.

———. *Cléomadès*. Ed. Albert Henry. Brussels: Editions de l'Université de Bruxelles, 1971. Vol. 5 (in 2 vols.) of *Les Oeuvres d'Adenet le Roi*.

———. *Les Enfances Ogier*. Ed. Albert Henry. Bruges: Rijksuniversiteit Te Gent, 1956. Vol. 3 of *Les Oeuvres d'Adenet le Roi*.

Ami et Amile: chanson de geste. Ed. Peter F. Dembowski. Paris: Librairie Honoré Champion, 1969.

Ami et Amile: A Medieval Tale of Friendship. Trans. Samuel N. Rosenberg and Samuel Danon. Ann Arbor: University of Michigan Press, 1996.

Aye d'Avignon: chanson de geste anonyme. Ed. S. J. Borg. Textes Littéraires français 34. Genève: Librairie Droz, S. A., 1967.

Béroul. *The Romance of Tristran*. Ed. and trans. Norris J. Lacy. Garland Library of Medieval Literature 36. New York: Garland Publishing Inc., 1989.

La Chanson d'Aspremont. Ed. Louis Brandin. 2 vols. Les Classiques Français du moyen âge. Paris: Champion, 1924.

La Chanson de Guillaume. Ed. Duncan McMillan. 2 vols. Paris: Editions A. et J. Picard, 1949.

La Chanson de Roland. Trans. Pierre Jonin. Paris: Editions Gallimard, 1979.

Chrétien de Troyes. *Le Chevalier de la charette*. Ed. and trans. Charles Méla. In *Chrétien de Troyes: Romans, suivis des Chansons, avec en appendice, Philoména*. Gen. ed. Michel Zink. Classiques Modernes: La Pochothèque. Turin: G. Canale, 1994.

Florence de Rome: chanson d'aventure du premier quart du XIIIe siècle. Paris: Librairie de Firmin-Didot, 1909.
Gormont et Isembart: Fragment de chanson de geste du XII siècle. Ed. Alphonse Bayot. Paris: Champion, 1931.
Gregory of Tours. *The Merovingians*. Ed. and trans. Alexander Callander Murray. Readings in Medieval Civilizations and Cultures 10. Peterborough, Ontario: Broadview Press, 2006.
The Knight of the Two Swords: A Thirteenth-Century Arthurian Romance. Trans. Ross G. Arthur and Noel L. Corbett. Gainesville: University Press of Florida, 1996.
Lancelot-Grail: The Old French Vulgate and Post-Vulgate in Translation: The Quest for the Holy Grail. Trans. E. Jane Burns. New York: Garland, 1995.
Libro de los huéspedes (Escorial MS H. I. B.): A Critical Edition. Ed. John K. Moore, Jr. MRTS 349. Tempe: Arizona Center for Medieval and Renaissance Studies, 2008.
Marie de France. *Lais*. Ed. and trans. Alexandre Micha. Paris: Flammarion, 1994.
The Pilgrimage of Charlemagne (Le Pèlerinage de Charlemagne). Ed. and trans. Glyn S. Burgess; *Aucassin et Nicolette (Aucassin et Nicolette)*. Ed. Anne Elizabeth Cobby. Trans. Glyn S. Burgess. Garland Library of Medieval Literature 47. New York: Garland Publishing, 1988.
Renart, Jean. *Galeran de Bretagne*. Ed. Lucien Foulet. Paris: Champion, 1925.
———. *L'Escoufle*. Ed. Franklin Sweetser. Geneva: Librairie Droz S. A., 1974.
Li Romans de Parise la duchesse. Ed. G. F. de Martonne. Paris: Techener, 1832–1848. Repr. Geneva: Slatkine Reprints, 1969.
Le Roman de Tristan en prose. Ed. Renée Curtis. Cambridge: D.S. Brewer, 1985.
The Song of Aspremont (La Chanson d'Aspremont). Trans. Michael A. Newth. Garland Library of Medieval Literature B 61. New York: Garland Publishing, Inc., 1989.
Villon, François. *Oeuvres: Traduction en français moderne accompagnée de notes explicatives*. Tome I, *Le Lais-Le Testament, Première partie*. Trad. André Lanly. Paris: Librairie Honoré Champion, 1978.
William, Count of Orange: Four Old French Epics. Trans. Glanville Price, Lynette Muir, and David Hoggan. London: J. M. Dent and Sons Ltd., 1975.

Secondary Works

Adler, Alfred. "Adenet's *Berte* and the Ideological Situation in the 1270's." *Studies in Philology* 45 (1948): 419–31.
Adnès, André. *Adenès, dernier grand trouvère: recherches historiques et anthroponymiques*. Paris: Editions A. et J. Picard, 1971.

Aebischer, Paul. *Des Annales carolingiennes à Doon de Mayence: nouveau recueil d'études sur l'épique française médiévale*. Publications romanes et françaises. Geneva: Librairie Droz S. A., 1975.

Aigrain, René. *L'hagiographie: ses sources, ses méthodes, son histoire*. Brussels: Société des Bollandistes, 2000.

The Benedictine Monks of Saint Augustine's Abbey, Ramsgate. *The Book of Saints*. London: A & C Black, 1989.

Black, Nancy B. *Medieval Narratives of Accused Queens*. Gainesville: University Press of Florida, 2003.

Burns, E. Jane. *Sea of Silk*. Philadelphia: University of Pennsylvania Press, 2009.

Calin, William C. *The Epic Quest: Studies in Four Old French* Chansons de geste. Baltimore: The Johns Hopkins University Press, 1966.

———. *The Old French Epic of Revolt*: Raoul de Cambrai, Renaud de Montauban, Gormond et Isembard. Geneva: Librairie Droz S. A., 1962.

Colliot, Régine. *Adenet le Roi: "Berte aus grans piés": Etude littéraire générale*. 2 vols. Paris: A. et J. Picard, 1970.

Coudenhove-Kalergi, Count Heinrich. *Anti-Semitism Throughout the Ages*. Ed. Count Richard Coudenhove-Kalergi. Trans. Angelo S. Rappoport. Westport, CT: Greenwood Press, 1972.

De Caluwé, Jacques. "Les Prières de *Berte aus grans piés* dans l'oeuvre d'Adenet le Roi." In *Mélanges de langue et de littérature médiévales offerts à Pierre le Gentil*, 151–60. Paris: S.E.D.E.S., 1973.

Duby, Georges. *Rural Economy and Country Life in the Medieval West*. Trans. Cynthia Postan. Columbia, SC: University of South Carolina Press, 1968.

Falk, Avner. *Anti-Semitism: A History and Psychoanalysis of Contemporary Hatred*. Westport, CT and London: Praeger Publishers, 2008.

Farmer, David Hugh. *The Oxford Dictionary of Saints*. Oxford: Oxford University Press, 1978.

Foehr-Janssens, Yasmina. "Une Reine au désert: désolation et majesté dans *Berte as grans piés* d'Adenet le Roi." In *L'Epopée romane au Moyen Age et aux temps modernes: Actes du XIV Congrès International de la Société Rencesvals pour l'étude des Épopées Romanes (Naples, 24–30 juillet 1997)*. ed. S. Luongo, 1: 229–45. 2 vols. Naples: Fredericiana Editrice Universitaria, 2001.

Goodrich, Norma Lorre. *Medieval Myths*. New York: The New American Library, 1961.

Green, Herman J. "The Pépin-Berte Saga and Philip I of France." *PMLA* 58 (1943): 911–19.

Gumpert, Matthew. *Grafting Helen: The Abduction of the Classical Past*. Madison: University of Wisconsin Press, 2001.

Hassell, James Woodrow, Jr. *Middle French Proverbs, Sentences, and Proverbial Phrases*. Toronto: Pontifical Institute of Mediaeval Studies, 1982.

Henry, Albert. *Biographie d'Adenet; La Tradition manuscrite.* Geneva: Slatkine Reprints, 1996. Vol. 1 of *Les Oeuvres d'Adenet le Roi.* 5 vols. Paris: Presses Universitaires de France, 1951–1970.

Herbermann, Charles G., et. al. eds. *The Catholic Encyclopedia.* 15 vols and index. New York: The Encyclopedia Press, Inc., 1913.

James-Raoul, Danièle. "Les Discours des mères: Aperçus dans les romans et lais du XIIe et XIII siècles." *Bien dire et bien aprandre* 16 (1998): 145–57.

Kay, Sarah. *The Chansons de geste in the Age of Romance: Political Fictions.* Oxford: Clarendon Press, 1995.

Kibler, William W. *Introduction to Old French.* New York: The Modern Language Association of America, 1984.

Krause, Kathy M., ed. *Reassessing the Heroine in Medieval French Literature.* Gainesville: University Press of Florida, 2001.

Lathuillère, Roger. *Guiron le Courtois: Etude de la tradition manuscrite et analyse critique.* Geneva: Librairie Droz S. A., 1966.

Lehmann, Andrée. *Le Rôle de la femme dans l'histoire de la France au moyen âge.* Paris: Editions Berger-Levrault, 1952.

Le Nan, Frédérique. "'Si li enuia mout la nuit. . .': Réflexion sur un élément commun de signification dans *Berte as grans piés* d'Adenet le Roi, le *Roman d'Alexandre* et la *Première Continuation de Perceval.*" *Revue des langues romanes* 106 (2002): 315–35.

Lives of the Desert Fathers (*The Historia Monachorum in Aegypto*). Trans. Russell Norman. Oxford and Kalamazoo: Mowbray and Cistercian Publications, 1981.

McBrien, Richard P. *The Lives of Saints.* San Francisco: HarperSanFrancisco, 2003

McGinn, Bernard. *Antichrist: Two Thousand Years of the Human Fascination with Evil.* San Francisco: HarperSanFrancisco, 1994.

———. *Visions of the End: Apocalyptic Traditions in the Middle Ages.* Records of Civilization: Sources and Studies 96. New York: Columbia University Press, 1979, repr. 1998.

Mancini, Mario. "Adenet gracieux et ambigu." *Cahiers de civilisation médiévale (Xe-XIIe siècles)* 17 (1974): 51–57.

Morawski, Joseph. *Proverbes français antérieurs au XVe siècle.* Paris: Champion, 1925.

Morgan, Leslie Zarker. "La regina tradita: Berta e Blançiflor nel ms. V13." In *La cultura dell'Italia padana e la presenza francese nei secoli XIII–XV: Pavia, 11–14 Sept. 1994,* 169–84. Alessandria: Edizioni dell'Orso, 2001.

———. "*Berta ai piedi grandi*: Historical Figure and Literary Symbol." *Olifant* 19 (1994–1995): 37–56.

Nebbiai-Dalla Guarda, Donatella. *La Bibliothèque de l'Abbaye de Saint-Denis en France du IXe au XVIIIe siècle.* Documents, études, et répertoires publiés par l'institut de recherche et d'histoire des textes. Paris: Editions du Centre National de la Recherche Scientifique, 1985.

Noble, Peter. "Saracen Heroes in Adenet le Roi." In *Romance Epic: Essays on a Medieval Literary Genre*, ed. Hans-Erich Keller, 189–201. Studies in Medieval Culture 24. Kalamazoo: Medieval Institute Publications, 1987.

Sismonde de Sismondi, J. C. L. *Histoire des Français*. 1850. Repr. as *The French under the Merovingians and Carolingians*. Trans. William Bellingham. New York: AMS Press, 1976.

Stanger, Mary D. "Literary Patronage at the Medieval Court of Flanders." *French Studies* 11 (1957): 214–29.

Vallet, Françoise. *De Clovis à Dagobert: les Mérovingiens*. Evreux: Gallimard/Réunion des musées nationaux, 1995.

Vance, Eugene. *Reading the Song of Roland*. Englewood Cliffs, NJ: Prentice-Hall, Inc., 1970.

Wolfgang, Leonora D. "Wilhelm Kellerman, 'Le Texte et la matière du roman *Berte aus grans piés* d'Adenet le Roi. À propos d'une nouvelle édition.' *Marche romane [Mélanges de philologie et de littératures romanes offerts à Jeanne Wathelet-Willem]* 28 (1978), pp. 287–300." *Olifant* 9 (1981): 77–78.

Wood, Ian N. *The Merovingian Kingdoms 450–751*. New York: Longman Publishing, 1994.

Bertha of the Big Foot

I

At the end of April, a mild and pretty time,
When little blades of grass spring up and the meadows grow green again
And bushes desire to be covered with flowers,
At this very moment the story I am telling you
Began in Paris on a Friday.   5
Since it was Friday, I decided
That I would go to Saint Denis to pray for God's mercy.
I became so well acquainted, I thank God for it,
With a courteous monk, one named Savari,
That he showed me the history book; and I saw there   10
The story of Bertha and also of Pépin,
How and in what way he assailed the lion.
Greenhorn minstrels and writers who didn't care enough to get the story right,
Who have from place to place here and there picked it up,
Have falsified the story so that I have never seen anything like it. 15
I stayed at Saint Denis from then until Tuesday,
Long enough that when I left I had the true story with me,
How Bertha was in the nearby forest
Where she endured many great pains and much suffering.
I will rhyme the story in such a way, by faith I swear to you,   20
That those who heretofore did not understand the story will be astounded.
And those who do understand will be happy.

II

At the time that I have begun the story for you,
There was a king in France of very great power,
Who was very cruel and fierce and savage in his warlike behavior.   25
Charles Martel was his name; he made many great invasions
Against Gerart and Foucon and those of their party.
They severed and separated many a soul from its body,
Broke many a hauberk, pierced many a buckler,

Battered down many a tower, destroyed many a city.   30
Then was peace so made and so established
That they were good friends without malice and without spite.
Then came the Vandals, an accursed race,
A people who appeared in great numbers and were full of false beliefs.
Then were their people killed and sent into exile.   35
I have collected other information for you.
Around the time of Saint John's Day when the rose is in bloom,
King Charles Martel was in his vaulted hall
In the city of Paris. He had many knights.
He had only two children; no one should contradict me in this.   40
One's name was Carloman; he was a good person.
Four years had he been a knight, full of courtesy;
And then he became a monk in an abbey.
The other was named Pépin, by God the Son of Mary.
He was five and a half feet tall, not a bit more;   45
But you never saw a more courageous person.
In the garden the king had many a table set up.
The king and his noble household had sat down to eat.
Elsewhere sat Pépin with his young men.
In the house was a lion that the family had had for a long time.   50
You never heard of a beast more cruel.
He had broken and totally destroyed his cage
And had killed his master, who was from Normandy.
Into the garden where there were many leafy plants
The lion came like a beast enraged.   55
He bit two young men from Lombardy
Who were playing on the lush grass.
Charles Martel jumped on it until he could no longer turn it away.
He led his wife away and did not leave her there,
Nor was there a single one of them who had not left the table.   60
When Pépin saw him, he flushed with rage,
He went into a room; his face was untroubled.
He found a javelin; he took it boldly in his hand.
He went toward the lion for good or for ill.

III

When Pépin held the sword, he did not want to delay.   65
He went toward the lion; he didn't feel like stopping.
Pépin nimbly went to him to give him such a blow;
He knew a spot on his chest to aim for.
Into the body he plunged the sword up to the hilt;

Into the body he made the cold steel pass. 70
He knocked him down to the ground; then the lion could not get up again.
Each one came running to look at the marvel.
Charles Martel himself ran to embrace his son,
And his mother began to weep with joy.
"My darling child," said she, "how did you dare to think 75
That you could approach so hideous a beast?"
"My lady," said Pépin, "one must not fear
A thing that one can dispose of with no blame."
Pépin was twenty years old, I've heard people say.
On this matter I no longer want to dwell. 80
I would like to go right to the heart of the true story
And briefly tell the matter and describe it.
You know well that we cannot last forever.
It is good to do good deeds; one cannot do more
Because all living creatures must come to an end 85
As did King Charles Martel.
Afterward his wife died, the queen with the fair face;
And so they crowned Pépin as rightful heir of France.
Afterward they married him off honorably.
His wife was related to Gerbert and Gerin 90
And Malvoisin the valiant, and I'm not lying.
With Fromont they had a war that you have heard about
During which many a soul was severed from its body.
Many a castle, many a tower was battered down.
Pépin had to endure great disasters because of it. 95
Never by this woman was he able to have a child
Because it did not please God, who watches over all.
They were together a long time; I couldn't tell you
All their adventures if I wanted to.
This lady died; may God save her soul! 100
Afterward they wanted Pépin to marry very soon.
For this reason the king assembled
All his trusted barons
To consider what wife they could advise him to take,
But they did not know where they could find him a wife. 105
Engerrans de Montcler spoke first:
"Sire, I know of one, by Saint Omer,
The daughter of the king of Hungary; much have I heard her praised.
There is no more beautiful woman on earth.
The noble Bertha, thus I have heard her called. 110
"My lords," said Pépin, "why delay?
This is the one I want as my wife and peer."

King Pépin had a great many people assemble
To go to Hungary to ask for the lady.
I don't want to enumerate to you all those who went.   115
Their path took them into Germany.
They had to go through many strange lands.
They arrived in Hungary on a Tuesday at dinnertime
At a great city, Strigon, I have heard it called.
There they found the king, who was a very praiseworthy man.   120
I do not want to tell you everything they said.
They went to ask for the young lady on behalf of Pépin,
And the king granted their request; he was glad to do it.
Blanchefleur the queen had them call her daughter.
The king had her shown to the French people,   125
And our French went decorously to greet her.
Her face, all white and rose, was lovely to see.
The tables were set; they sat down to dinner.
As long as they were there, the king and the queen
Impressed them as being very honorable.   130
They did not want to stay there long.
As soon as they could, they prepared to depart.
Horses, gold and silver were presented to them
But they refused to take as much as a penny's worth.

IV

Gentle Bertha, who never had a mean thought,   135
Was crying very hard as she took leave of her father.
"Sire," she said, "adieu! Say goodbye for me to my brother
Who holds the land of Grodno near Poland."
"Daughter," said the king, "be like your mother.
Do not be either hateful or pitiless toward the poor   140
But kind and noble and good-natured
So that your goodness is evident to God and to the world,
For he who acts like this glorifies himself most nobly,
And he who does not pays the price in the end.
Never has a king or emperor seen a more beautiful girl than you.   145
I commend you to God, who is the true ruler.
May he in all ways be the guardian of your body and soul."

V

Right at the time that I am telling you about
There was a custom in the Germanic countries
That all the great lords, counts and marquises 150
Had French people speaking French all around them
In order to teach French to their sons and daughters.
The king and the queen and Bertha of the fair face
Knew Parisian French nearly as well as if
They had been born in the city or in Saint Denis 155
Because the king of Hungary was brought up in France.
He was taken there from his country when he was very small.
Aliste knew French because she had learned it in the palace.
She was the servant's daughter, may she be dishonored,
For later through her were many very evil deeds undertaken. 160
Thus the French considered the Germanic people friends.
They helped one another against the Arabs.
It certainly seemed later on to Charles, who was a powerful king,
That the Germans were knights of great worth.
They killed and conquered many Turks then. 165
I'll tell you no long stories about this.
I want to talk to you about the matter I have undertaken.

VI

Bertha was very courteous and full of noble character.
No one knew her who did not greatly esteem her.
The day that she was to undertake her journey 170
She knelt before her father, King Flore.
Weeping, she took leave of him without bitterness and without pretense.
Bertha was as rosy-cheeked and as pleasing as you could wish for.
There was no more beautiful girl from here to Pisa,
And she greatly desired to act nobly in all things. 175
Therefore, she was never reproached with any misdeed.
But she was mistreated in the forest by the servant
As you will later hear the story tell.

VII

When Bertha had taken leave of her father of the true heart,
Her heart grieved hard; she was greatly overwrought. 180
The people of that land, I won't lie to you,
Cried a great deal; I know they did.

"Daughter," said the queen, "know that I shall go with you,
As far as I can.
I'll leave you with our servant Margiste 185
And Aliste her daughter, the most beautiful girl I know;
For she looks like you and is that much dearer to me because of it.
I will send their cousin Tybert with them.
You know very well that I freed each of them from serfdom
And that I bought the freedom of each one of them with my money, 190
And that for that reason I have even more faith in them."
"And, my lady," said Bertha, "I will love them, too;
And I will never deprive them of anything I have.
I will conduct every one of my private affairs with their advice.
I will see that Aliste is married very well if I can." 195
"Daughter," said the queen, "I will be very grateful to you for it."
One Monday morning, I'm telling you the truth,
They put Bertha on a bay palfrey.
I'm not going to go into detail about their travels.
They came to Saxony to Duke Nicholai's. 200
The duchess was Bertha's sister (I found all this
When I read the story at Saint Denis).
I'll not delay getting to this task any longer.
"Daughter," Blanchefleur said, "I shall go back now.
I'll greet your father warmly on your behalf. 205
If you do not do well, I shall die of grief.
I shall take this ring from your finger away with me.
Weeping and grieving, I shall kiss it often."
Weeping, Bertha said to her, "My lady, I shall give it to you."

VIII

Bertha took off the ring, for she could not delay doing so any longer. 210
She gave it to her mother, weeping profusely, very distressed.
"Daughter, I commend you to God by whom the sun shines.
Now make yourself beloved by the lettered and the unlettered alike.
It is right that one who has come from goodness go toward goodness,
Always doing better and better, therefore never departing from the good." 215
"Dear mother," said she, "I feel as though
A knife had been plunged into my heart."
"Daughter," said the queen, "be joyous and merry.
You are going to France; my heart is comforted by that,
For in no country are the people kinder or truer." 220
At the departure, everyone began to weep again:
Bertha fell in a faint on a cloth black as a nun's habit.

IX

The queen went away in accordance with the will of God.
Bertha remained in a swoon on the pavement.
The duchess her sister took her in her arms. 225
Blanchefleur grieved so that her heart nearly broke.
She went back to Hungary where the king awaited her.
Our French people had gotten their baggage ready.
Bertha of the noble heart took leave of her sister.
Her people put her gently on the palfrey. 230
They crossed Germany; they did not linger there.
At Saint Herbert they rapidly crossed the Rhine.
They rode through the Ardennes without any delay.
They took lodging at Rostemont on the Meuse
In a very rich castle seated most nobly. 235
It was set between two rivers in lordly fashion
Among forests and meadows; of these it lacked nothing.
Afterwards Duke Namles of Bavaria remodeled it differently
Than it had been and much more strongly,
For Namles was full of great courage. 240
He was worthy and loyal and wise and knowledgeable.
Later the place was commonly called Namur.
The count lodged them most honorably.
He was a cousin to King Flore, to whom Hungary belongs.
He made many rich presents to our French people. 245
But never did they take horses, gold or silver.
They left Rostemont merrily in the morning.
They went through Hainaut, Vermandois also.
I will not prolong this any more for you.
Right on a Sunday, as I have heard it, 250
They came to Paris at twilight.
The king came to meet them very joyously;
And more than one thousand seven hundred were with him,
Every one of whom held great fiefs from him.
They went to greet Bertha graciously and courteously, 255
As, wise and courteous, she returned the greeting to each one
Like someone who was very thoughtful.
One said to the other, "By Saint Clement,
Indeed, we have a lady who is beautiful and quite young."
The bells of the city rang loudly. 260
I do not want to give you a long account of this,
For there was not a street in the city, to my knowledge,
That was not all very richly covered with cloth;

And the streets were strewn very cleanly with grass.
And ladies dressed in finery for the arrival 265
Danced and made merry and sang loudly.
All Paris was resplendent with jewels and riches.
The queen descended onto the steps of the palace.
Many high barons accompanied her with much courtesy
Because each one had a great desire to honor her. 270

X

After mid-August, I don't want to mislead you,
On such a beautiful day that it was neither raining or windy,
King Pépin married the noble Bertha.
She was richly dressed in a rich cloth of Otranto.
She had a crown on her head that greatly became her. 275
It was worth a hundred thousand marks and more, at a fair sale.
Bertha was as gracious as the flower on the stem.
Everyone thought she was beautiful; no one disagreed with that.
They had the master pavilion set up in the garden.
When the mass was said, they did not wait long. 280
They sat down to eat, here one hundred, there twenty, there thirty.
Many a great prince presented himself to wait on her that day.
Before the queen was many a noble youth
Who would gladly have served her; there were none who did not desire to.
She was quite content then, but soon she would be grieving. 285
Margiste would make her receive such treatment,
By her very great evil would put her in such a path
That often her face would be quite wet with tears.
May the Lord God destroy her, the stinking old piece of filth!

XI

They removed the tablecloths after the meal. 290
Minstrels prepared to play,
Three minstrels who were greatly esteemed.
They did not want to wait; they came before the king
And the queen to entertain her.
One played the hurdy-gurdy: his name was Gautier. 295
And the other was a harpist: his name was Master Garnier.
The other played the lute; he was very skilled at it.
I do not know what his name was; I do not want to lie to you.
The ladies and knights heard them gladly.
When they had finished playing, they retreated to the back. 300

Then the king got up; he did not want to wait any longer.
Ladies and young gentlemen took to making merry.
You would have seen them begin various sorts of dances.
Duke and count and prince accompanied the queen.
They led her into her chambers so that she might rest. 305
Then they went on back; they did not want to linger.
They did not want to impose for too long on the queen.
And suddenly there was Margiste; may God hinder her.
She already had the thought of the devil in her heart,
For she had already devised a very deadly attack. 310
She went to kneel beside the queen.
At once she began to whisper in her ear:
"My lady, I am terribly sad, by Saint Richier.
A friend of mine came to me yesterday evening to tell me
That since God let his body be crucified 315
There is no man alive who is as much to be feared
As King Pépin, whom you are going to lie down beside.
When the king must have marital relations with you tonight
And exercise the rights that one has with his wife,
I am afraid that he might kill you, God help me. 320
I've known it for a good while; I did not dare to tell you
Because I did not want to frighten you too much."
When the queen heard this, she began to cry.
She was so afraid that she thought she would lose her mind.
"My lady," said the old woman, "don't worry. 325
I will protect you well, by the just God.
When the bishop and the abbot come back from blessing
The bed of King Pépin, who has France to govern,
I will have everyone leave your room.
I will have my daughter Aliste undress right away. 330
I will have her hide in the bed in place of you.
I have spoken to her; I have had her agree to it.
I'd rather have her die than you; I won't lie to you."
When Bertha heard this, she embraced her.
She began to thank the Lord God and his saints. 335
She would not have been at all happier if she had been given the gold of Montpellier.

XII

The queen became very joyous when she heard the way
That she would be able to hold herself back from King Pépin.
She thanked our Lady, the just Lady.

The evil chambermaid left her.   340
The filthy old witch went into another room
Near the garden of the king, quite close to the river.
There she found her daughter—may she be struck dead—
At a little window which was made of stone.
She resembled Bertha more than any portrait a painter could paint.   345
Their beauty was great; no other woman's equaled it
Any more than a meadow in flower resembles a wasteland of brush.
Suddenly, there was the old woman, whose face was most joyous.
She embraced her daughter and kissed her on the face.
The old woman and her daughter had plotted   350
How they could betray Bertha and in what way.
"Daughter," said the old woman, "I love you dearly,
For you shall be queen if it please God and Saint Peter."
"Mother," said Aliste, "may God hear your prayer!
Send for Tybert. I think   355
That he should be master and counselor in this matter.
Send him word to come to me. Let him be sought for quickly
On the pretext that he had my almsbag last evening and needs to return it."
And the old woman herself ran there like a greyhound.
She was not a bit reluctant to carry out the betrayal.   360

XIII

When Tybert heard the message, he very much wanted
To go quickly to his cousin.
And when he had come, they soon made him assent
To this treason. He agreed to it with pleasure.
They planned the treason among the three of them at leisure,   365
How and in what manner they could make it come about that
They could take France away from Bertha, their lady.
"Daughter," said the mother, "I won't lie to you:
A person must back up quite a bit to take the longest jump.
You will have to suffer a little bit because of this thing.   370
Tonight I shall have Bertha sleep with me.
Right at dawn, when it starts to get light,
I shall send her to you as if she were going to lie down in that bed.
You must then strike such a blow in your thigh
That the bright blood will gush out   375
Because of which you will cry out, 'Help,' that she wants to murder you.
I shall enter the chamber and seize her at once.
Let me manage things from that point on."
"My lady," said the servant, "whatever you wish."

Thus they planned it. May God shame them! 380
That night after supper, when evening was coming on,
The bishop and the abbot went to bless the bed.
Afterwards, the old woman made all the people leave.
She had them go out one after another in orderly fashion.
She darkened the room so that nothing could be seen in it. 385
She had her daughter cover up in King Pépin's bed.
They put the knife with which they would do the treason
Right on the edge of the bed. May God curse them!

XIV

The old woman was very happy. She started laughing with joy.
She went into her chamber to say to her lady Bertha, 390
"My lady, I left my daughter sad and full of anger.
We have done more for you than anyone could tell."
"My lady, you are telling the truth. May God reward you for it!"
The old woman had her go to bed. May God send great suffering
To her, her daughter, and Tybert. May all evil visit them. 395
The old woman told her quietly, step by step,
That right at daybreak she must get ready
And very discreetly go to the king.
Gentle Bertha without anger and without malice
Said that she would do that. She had no wish to refuse. 400
She did not want to contradict anything the old woman wanted.
Sitting in her bed, she began to say her prayers,
For she was well-educated and could write well.

XV

That night the king did all he wished
With the very false servant, full of evil. 405
In truth, he engendered an heir
Who had the name of Rainfrois and had scarcely any goodness in him.
Later he had another one by her; they called him Heudris.
They were full of malice and great falsity.
Before the dawn appeared, just at the point of day, 410
The old woman sent for Tybert the traitor,
And he came willingly and gladly.
Bertha awakened and stayed there no more.
She entered into the chamber quietly and softly,
Just as the old woman had told her to. 415
She went to the servant, who lay on the beautifully appointed bed.

The servant saw her and waited no longer.
She seized the knife, raised it high,
And in the back of her thigh struck such a blow
That the bright blood flowed from it everywhere. 420
The servant held out the knife to Bertha,
And Bertha took it without suspicion;
For the old woman had thus completely deceived her.
Then the evil servant let out a great cry:
"Ha! King Pépin," said she, "I believe you were born in an evil hour 425
When someone wants to murder me right by your side."
And the king woke up; he saw the knife
That the queen was holding all covered with blood.
He sat up, nearly out of his mind,
And behold! Here was the old woman, who pretended to be angry. 430
She went toward her daughter and looked at the blood.
When the king saw her, she swore to God
That her daughter had to be destroyed; never would that be changed.
"Ha! King," said the old woman, "for holy charity,
Have her killed right away; have no pity on her. 435
Never will I love her a day of my life."
The old woman took Bertha and gave her a great blow.
She pushed her from the chamber. Bertha went willingly.
She still believed that this was friendship;
And, nevertheless, her eyes were tearing from the blow. 440
And Tybert seized her. May he have a horrible fate.
He pulled her along by the coat in such a way that he tore it.
"Help, God," cried Bertha, "king full of humility!
What has happened to me? What are these people thinking of?"
Then the evil old woman went on ahead a bit. 445
She reached for a rope and gave it to Tybert.
They struck Bertha and did not stop.
They opened her mouth violently
And put a rope on her the way one would bridle a horse.
This was a great cruelty. 450
At the nape of the neck, they made such a knot
That for one hundred thousand marks she could not have uttered a word.
They bound up her hands by their treachery.
They threw her down on a bed and threw a sheet over her.
Now may God, the king of majesty, have pity on her! 455

XVI

When they had bound Bertha up in such a way
That the cord was very tightly knotted in her mouth
And they had thrown her across the bed,
The old woman came up close to her.
She whispered in her ear so no one else would hear: 460
"If you cry out, by the honored Virgin,
You will have your head cut off immediately."
When Bertha heard this, she was terrified.
She saw well that they had betrayed her and that she had been deceived.
She fainted then from suffering and pain. 465
And the old woman turned away; she didn't stay any longer.
She left Tybert with Bertha so that she would be well guarded.
The old woman went into the king's room.
She acted very sad and seemed angry.
When she saw where her daughter was, she went to her. 470
"My lady, have mercy, for God who made the heaven and the dew,
If you saw what I have done to my daughter
You would certainly say that I am not guilty in this plot."
"Shut your mouth," said the king, "you proven old whore.
Your treason has been seen and witnessed. 475
You wanted to murder Bertha, my wife, in secret.
Your daughter will be burned; that decision will never be altered."
"My lord," said Aliste, "I would never have thought
That any treason was plotted by this person.
There is not a worthier woman from here to the Betee Sea. 480
But her daughter has always been a confirmed fool,
Acting like a lunatic or like someone insane.
My lord, I request a favor of you this morning.
It is the first thing I have asked of you
Since you have, my lord, taken me as your wife 485
And I was crowned in front of you with a golden crown.
I implore you on the faith that you have sworn me
That this thing be so hushed up and hidden
That no man born of woman will know it.
Because I brought her with me, 490
I would be too chagrined if it were talked about.
Instead take three men at arms right this very morning.
Let the strumpet be given to them as quickly as possible.
Let her be taken immediately to a far country.
Let her be buried where she is strangled. 495
I don't care what they do with her as long as she is killed."

"My lady," said the old woman, "you have thought this out well.
By my soul I would want her to have her head cut off
Or be drowned or go to the devil."
The king heard the request; he did not refuse it.　　　　　　　　500
On the contrary, he granted and agreed to all of it.
The servant worked at it so and made such an effort
That the old woman her mother agreed with the king
To carry out the whole thing.
With joy the old woman bowed before the king.　　　　　　　　505
Her face showed great distress and was covered with tears.
She had carried out the treason quite well and fashioned it expertly.

XVII

The king stood up; he didn't want to stay any longer,
For he was in great haste to see this thing accomplished.
He himself went to call three men at arms,　　　　　　　　　　510
But he did not want to explain to them anything about the business.
He led them to Margiste and told them
That they should do all she wanted without hesitation.
"My lord," the old woman said, "you go on back
And I will get this thing completely ready,　　　　　　　　　　515
And then I will tell you what I want to order done."
She showed them the chamber where Bertha was.
"Bring her back here to me; you need to hurry."
Then the old woman turned away; she did not want to linger there.
She took leave of the king, and began to sigh.　　　　　　　　　520
From the way she was acting, it seemed that she must be going crazy.
Weeping, she called out to the king:
"My lord, go back to bed. You may be sure
That you will never hear anything about her again.
I no longer consider her my daughter, truly I can swear it,　　　　525
Since she wants to murder or strangle my lady."
Then the old woman departed; may God destroy her!
And the servant her daughter started crying profusely.
Just as if she were grieving, she took to sighing.
The king was very courteous; he began to comfort her.　　　　　530
"My beauty," said the king, "leave off this grieving.
Let the strumpet go; may God give her evil!
She could very well have killed you or poisoned you.
Are you hurt much? You ought not to hide anything from me."
"No, my lord," says she, "This doesn't hurt.　　　　　　　　　535
Seeing my blood frightened me.

I'll show it to you; go close the door."
She said all this to distract him,
To have more time to carry out their business.
And Tybert and the old woman had no desire to stop.   540
Thus they had their lady Bertha put up on a pack horse.
The three men at arms took her away right after daybreak,
And Tybert was the fourth. May God save Bertha;
May he deliver her from this great peril!
The old woman took her cousin Tybert aside to ask   545
That he bring her back the heart; this he did not want to forget.
The old lady began to counsel him well,
How he must take charge of the treason
And how Bertha should be guarded so that she could not talk.
"My lady," Tybert said, "rest assured that   550
I will do the job well; never doubt it."
He took leave of the old woman. They began their journey.

XVIII

After dawn appeared, the moon shone brightly.
By it they led Bertha, who was going toward great misfortune.
She was full of faith and good character.   555
They had covered her well so that she could not be seen.
"Ha! Lord God," she said, "who art the sovereign Father,
I am going to be punished although I have not merited it.
Alas! What evil and pitiless people I have found!
Is there any misfortune in the world that compares to mine?   560
Alas! I shall never again see my sweet, dear mother
Nor King Flore my father, my sister or my brother.
Now may God be guardian of my body and soul!"

XIX

Bertha was very sad; I don't want to lie to you.
She called on the Lord God, the just Father.   565
She did not know where they were leading her, forward or backward.
I do not want to tell you in detail about all their travel.
When they came to a lodging, Tybert put Bertha
In a room or high chamber; he did not let anyone approach her
Except himself alone; may God hinder him!   570
And when he gave her food and drink,
In his fist he held his unsheathed sword of polished steel
Because he wanted to frighten her so much

That she would not say a word or make any noise.
He did not want to be away from her at any time. 575
Then he put the rope in her mouth again.
Then he tied her hands like a filthy traitor.
He had her locked up until dawn.
That is they way they traveled—I am not lying—
For five whole long days—they did not want to delay— 580
Until they came to a great, high, dense wood.
It was the forest of Le Mans, I have heard said.
Then they stopped under an olive tree.
"My lord," said Tybert, "by Saint Richier,
We don't need to go any farther." 585
And they answered him, "We agree."
Then they all got down to the ground, on the grass.
One of them was named Moran—he was highly esteemed—
And the other Godefrois; the third was called Renier.
They dismounted the queen; may God help her now! 590
They could never get near enough to touch her
Because Tybert would not let anyone but himself approach her.
They had her take off all the coverings over her clothes.
She wore a white tunic and a very costly coat.
When they saw that she was so beautiful, they started to cry; 595
And Tybert, the traitor, drew his sword.
"My lords," said Tybert, "get back now.
With one blow I'm going to cut off her head."
When Bertha saw the sword, she started to bend over.
From fear she lay down with her face to the ground. 600
Then she began to kiss the earth sweetly.
She could not tell them her great misfortune
Because the rope in her mouth would not let her speak.
"Tybert," said Moran,"don't strike her,
For by the holy Lord who has all to govern, 605
Forthwith you will see your arms and legs and head cut off
If ever I return to France."

XX

That day the weather was cold and raw,
And Bertha lay face down on the ground upon the heather.
She was afraid that Tybert would strike her. 610
She called on our Lady, the good Lady.
"My lords," Moran said, "I think that the one who would look

Upon such a noble young girl with evil intent would be a very base person."
"By God," said Tybert, "I swear I think that
We should kill her soon and then go back. 615
For I have promised Margiste, whom I hold dear."
"Tybert," said Moran, "you have a heart as hard as stone.
If you do her any harm, by Saint Peter the Apostle,
All the gold of Bavaria would not guarantee you
That this woods will not be your bed forever." 620

XXI

Tybert the thief had a very angry heart
When he was not allowed to kill Bertha.
Nevertheless, the traitor brandished his polished sword;
And the three men of arms grabbed him by the flanks
So that he was forced to kneel on the ground. 625
Each one drew his sword; they didn't hesitate.
While the two of them held Tybert the traitor,
Moran, who had great compassion, untied Bertha.
He did not neglect to take the rope out of her mouth.
"Fair one, run away from here; don't wait any longer. 630
The Lord God guide you with his sweet love!"
Bertha ran away; her heart was frightened,
For she had thought for certain she would have her head cut off.
She fled into the forest, thanking God greatly.
Thus Bertha escaped Tybert without his leave. 635
When Tybert saw this, he was very angry.
"My lord," said Tybert, "you have done a great evil.
I will have you all hanged when you return."

XXII

That day the weather was very bad, for it rained and there was lightning.
Bertha ran away by the side of a clearing. 640
She ran so far that the men at arms lost sight of her.
"My lord," said Moran, "may God have sway over me,
We did a terrible thing
When we came here to do such a murder.
She certainly seems to be a noble woman and without any evil ways. 645
May the Lord God guide her and protect her!
In this forest are many a bear and many a leopard
That will not wait long to eat her.

We treated her as a criminal or a traitor would.
My heart aches through and through with sadness and pity."   650
At these words they got back on their horses; they all left.

XXIII

In the forest Bertha hid in the bushes.
May the Lord God and all his holy names counsel her!
We'll leave off talking to you about her here.
At the proper time and place, we'll resume telling about her.   655
The men at arms went back; they did not make any stops.
"My lords," Moran said, "do you know what we will do?
I recommend that we take back the heart of a pig.
We will present it to my lady Margiste.
In this way we shall certainly avoid censure.   660
And you know very well all that we agreed with her to do,
That we were supposed to bring back that girl's heart."
"Tybert," said Moran, "by Saint Simon,
If you do not agree to this, we shall kill you."
"My lords," said Tybert, "this counsel is very good.   665
Since she has escaped, we'll make the best of it.
I am more afraid than you. I tell you openly
That we will be accused of this thing."
Each one swore an oath; the vow was short.
We will not linger on this matter.   670
They did everything we've told you.
They came to Paris; we won't lie to you.
The old lady was very joyous when she heard what they had to say.
"My lady," said Tybert, "we have brought you back
The heart; here it is; we are making a gift of it to you.   675
We killed the girl; we are telling you the truth."
"My lord," the old woman said, "we are well rewarded.
There has never been so evil a strumpet for as long as the world has existed."

XXIV

The three men at arms went away; none of them lingered.
They came to their lodging; they all went in,   680
And Tybert and the old woman stayed there.
They went upstairs together to the false queen.
She was very joyous that Tybert had come back.
"My lady," said Tybert, "something good has happened for you.
We killed Bertha with our sharp swords."   685

"Tybert," said Aliste, "Jesus be praised for it.
You have certainly deserved my friendship."
Thus was Tybert gleefully answered by the servant
Because her heart was moved with great joy.
I have never before heard spoken of such a betrayal   690
Since our Lord was sold by Judas.
May the Lord God who was crucified for us
Grant that they may yet get their just deserts!
King Pépin had received the Hungarians well
And given them many rich gifts nobly presented.   695
They traveled so much that they had all returned to their country.
They greeted Flore and Blanchefleur on behalf of Pépin
And on behalf of the filthy servant, may she be destroyed!
I will leave off talking of them; I'll say no more about them now.
I shall return to Bertha, who in the branchy woods   700
Was in very great distress; her heart was desperately troubled.
She called often upon God and his holy powers.
She did not know which way to turn. She kept on making her way farther
From the place where Tybert, the deceiver, had left her.

XXV

The lady was in the woods, crying bitterly.   705
She heard the owls hoot and the wolves howl.
There was much lightning and loud thunder.
It was raining steadily and hailing and the wind was blowing.
It was a frightful situation for a lady all by herself.
She called softly upon the Lord God and all his saints: 710
"Ha! Lord God," said she, "it is true that this happened:
You were born of the Virgin. When the star appeared,
The three kings sought for you. There will never be a man
Whom you deprive of protection the day that he calls upon them.
Melchior was the name of the one who brought myrrh.   715
Jaspar was the name of the other one who gave you incense.
And Balthazar was the third, who presented gold to you.
Lord, you took it; each one kneeled.
As true as this was, God, and it is true, I'm not lying,
So protect this weary one who is going mad."   720
When she had finished her prayer, she pulled up her coat,
Commended herself to God, and went away into the woods.

XXVI

Bertha moved on quickly following the slope of a valley.
She called upon God, the spiritual Father,
Him and his sweet Mother, so that they would protect her from evil.   725
She did not know what she could do; her heart was filled with grief.
"Ah! old woman," said she, "you had a disloyal heart
To betray me like this with such cruel treachery.
Alas! What a burdensome day I will have suffered today!
It hardly seems that I am of royal lineage.   730
May God and Saint Julien send me to a place
Where no evil beast can eat me;
For my heart is firmly, tenderly and loyally entrusted to God."

XXVII

That day the queen endured fatigue and terrible suffering.
She had neither pack horses with coffers nor trunks filled with bedclothing,   735
Nor house to lodge in, nor vaulted chamber nor palace.
She grieved more than one who is sinking into the ocean.
There was no finer lady from here to Thessaly,
Not to my knowledge from here to Wales.
But she was fatigued; she was a little pale from it.   740
Now you should know that she had no desire to dance.
From the bad weather her clothes were a little heavy and dirty.
She found a river which descended from a hillside.
She would have gladly drunk some, but it was murky like beer.

XXVIII

Through the woods went the lady, who was very much afraid.   745
It's no great wonder if her heart was in pain
As one must be who does not know where to go.
She often looked to the right and the left
And in front and behind, and then stopped.
When she stopped, she would cry most tenderly.   750
She often would kneel on her bare knees on the ground.
She often lay down with arms extended on the lush grass.
She often piteously kissed the earth.
When she got up, she heaved many a great sigh.
She lamented her mother, Blanchefleur the queen.   755
"Ha! madame," she said, "if you knew now
What trouble I am in, your heart would break."

Then she would put her hands together and extend them toward God.
"This Lord God," said she, "who sits high and sees far,
May he lead me through this forest today   760
And may his very dear Mother accompany me to a place
Where my body might not be put to shame!"
Then she sat down under a tree, for her heart was growing weary.
She often wrung her very beautiful white hands.
She often commended herself to God and to his Mother.   765

XXIX

In the forest was Bertha, who was gentle and upright.
She tried her best to go down out of the woods,
For she so badly wanted to be in the fields.
But the path meandered frequently and was narrow.
She did not know where to go to find the straightest way.   770
"Oh! Old woman," said she, "very evil and treacherous,
Why did you send me in great haste and on the sly
Into this forest, in exile, in secret?
I fear the hour that beasts will attack me here.
You have thrown me into pain and suffering.   775
May God and his Mother curse you.
Ah! Lord God," said she, "what a bad prospect I face!
My heart is full of pain and fear;
And therefore help me, blessed Mother of God."

XXX

Blanchefleur's daughter, the queen with the fair face,   780
Was in the forest; her heart was heavy.
She was the daughter of King Flore, who was valiant and noble.
If he had known of this calamity, he would have been greatly distressed.
She had a sister whose name was Aelis,
The wife of the duke of Saxony; and so he was count and marquis.   785
He held the land of Brandenburg.
Bertha was of very high lineage, that I guarantee you,
Of kings, emperors, and excellent princes.
She was sitting under a tree, disconsolate.
She was as red as a rose, as white as a lily.   790
"Ah! God, will I never see my friends?
Woe is me! Tired, sad, how my body is punished,
Suffering and chagrined, outraged and afflicted,
Poor and abandoned, exiled and dispossessed!

Ah! God, I thought I had risen to very high esteem 795
When I was given Pépin, who is a powerful king,
And I was taken to the city of Paris.
But I see truly; and so it seems to me
That my situation is always going from bad to worse."
Piteously, she crossed her arms on her bosom. 800

XXXI

The lady was in the woods seated beneath a tree.
She was dressed in a tunic over her bodice.
She had on a coat trimmed with costly gray fur,
And the cloth was made in the kingdom of Leutice.
She certainly seemed like a noblewoman; her appearance was very 805
    distinguished.
But her heart was weary; she was not cowardly,
For the rain and the wind had beaten her so,
And the hail had fallen on her clothing
So that she had dropped down in a faint on the gray stone.
When the fainting came upon her, she undertook to speak. 810
She commended herself to God and to Saint Denis:
"Alas that my father, the king full of noble character, may not know
That without deserving it I have encountered such misfortune
And that in this forest I am so alone and abandoned!
I know very well that he would already be looking for me. 815
He would have me sought from Spain to Friesland,
But I do not know by what means or in what manner
He would ever learn any news of me.
I commend myself to God
Who died on the cross to redeem sinners; so as I love and esteem him 820
May he protect me from shame so that I am not mistreated
Nor devoured nor caught by a wild beast."

XXXII

Bertha was in the woods seated under a beech tree
On a stream called the Minclo.
She could not cross over it without getting wet. 825
"Ah! Lord God," she said, "I dedicate my heart to you.
May it please you that my body and soul and whatever I have be yours.
As one who seeks to serve you in all things, I pledge myself."
She hit a pebble so hard

That it wounded her foot through her shoe 830
So that it was bleeding as if it had been pierced with a nail.
"Ah me! Alas," she said, "I would cry out for help,
But I dare not because of the beasts that I hear howling in these woods.
I can say 'halt' to going where good will come to me.
I am cold wrapped up in my coat. 835
But whatever distress I have, I still praise God in it.
Ha, King Pépin," she said, "I do not share your wealth.
You have much and I have too little."

XXXIII

Bertha lay on the ground, which was hard as a rock.
There was not a more beautiful woman from there to the Danube. 840
She was well-mannered and courteous, did not grimace or pout.
Someone had made a little seat there.
The beauty, who had begun to cry, leaned against it;
For she was limping with pain like a horse that has nails in its feet.
As she fled, the briars made many a rag 845
Of her dress, and the lady wrapped them around her.
Her color was not like an owl's.
She was as white as chalk that one hoes
Mixed with red and polished like a peacock.
A branch had scratched her on the right cheek 850
So harshly that the flesh was blue from it.
From effort and pain she was extremely weak and languishing;
But whatever she had to suffer, she praised God and his Mother for it
Softly, so that no beast would hear her speaking.
Often in her distress her misfortunes become more painful to her. 855
"Ah, Fortune," said she, "how you have frowned upon me!
The wheel of Fortune turns inconstantly for me
When from such high honor I have fallen in the mud.
I am not as comfortable as a fish at ease in the water.
I feel like a finch or a lark 860
That a hungry sparrowhawk holds seized in its beak,
For I fear a time when a bear or a lion
Might hold me in its teeth or claws and tear me apart.
God, if as you know I am completely devoted to you,
Grant that your Mother love me with her love given 865
So lovingly that it may never leave me,
So that I am enveloped in it in paradise,
For from the hands of the devil she releases many a sinner."

XXXIV

There was much violent weather this overcast day;
And the queen cried, who was suffering and had suffered 870
Great hardship and great pain, but she bore it with an open heart
In accordance with the will of God and faithfully served him;
For the one who does so deserves paradise for it.
"God!" she said, "If only my mother of the sincere heart
Knew that she is losing her daughter Bertha in this forest! 875
My father the king had very foolish and deceptive advice
Who burdened me with the old woman and her cousin Tybert.
God grant me such vengeance that their evil betrayal
Be yet discovered before all in the open.
When I crossed the Rhine right at Saint Herbert 880
I did not believe I would take my lodging here."

XXXV

In the forest of Le Mans was Queen Bertha,
And the night was horrible and terrifying.
Her head and face were scarcely covered,
And the queen suffered greatly from the cold. 885
She was right in the wildest part of the forest.
She had nothing except little bushes where she sheltered herself from the wind.
In her trials she was very enterprising.
She wiped her sweet face with her tunic.
She called upon Saint Barbara, who was a true convert, 890
And Saint Katherine. "Each one was offered up to
God in great martyrdom and had from it such recompense
That the true door of paradise was opened for her.
So I must bear it willingly if I am cold and poor.
God, if just in believing in you I am complete and true and assured, 895
Protect me so that I am not taken by a vile beast
Nor eaten in this wood nor brought to destruction."

XXXVI

Lords, now listen, I don't want to bore you, for heaven's sake,
But hear a true story of which the verses are well written.
All ladies and gentlemen should hear it most willingly; 900
For there are very few, in my opinion,
Which approach this one with authenticity.
I have my guarantee at Saint Denis in France

Where I found the story within a book on a shelf.
The day was waning; thus night was approaching.   905
When the queen saw this, she fled into the deep woods,
Into a place that the beasts had made and prepared.
Bushes, maybe seven or eight of them, were there.
She was very frightened by the wind, which was making too great a noise.
She often commended herself to the guidance of the Lord God.   910
She had nothing that she could eat, either raw or cooked,
Neither bread nor meat nor wine nor cake nor twice-cooked food.
She bent over a little, for she was growing weak.
You should know that she had scarcely any joy or pleasure,
The queen who would later carry the noble fruit   915
Who was the cause of the death and destruction of many a Saracen.

XXXVII

When the lady saw that night was falling in the woods
And that the twilight was treacherous and deceiving,
Against the wind she made herself a shield of bushes, which was a great struggle.
"God," said she, "how I have been deceived and led astray!   920
Laughter and comfort and joy have certainly abandoned me.
In this forest I am having a miserable time.
I believe that beasts have made this hidden shelter,
For it is, it seems to me, very strangely fashioned.
I do not see that my fate is improving;   925
For if they find me, I am dead and destroyed.
They will sooner eat me raw than cooked
As willingly as the wolf does the trout.
God can very well protect me, who led me here.
I shall remain in this place; I see no other way out."   930

XXXVIII

The lady had poor lodging when night fell.
She had neither house nor hall nor room nor attic,
Nor mattress nor cushion, bedclothing nor pillow,
Nor lady nor girl, nor man-at-arms nor squire,
Nor rug spread out to comfort her.   935
She called upon the Lord God, the just Father.
She made a little mound of olive leaves,
For she thought she would close her eyes briefly.
But if Jesus, who has all to govern, had not taken care of her
She would soon have had calamitous trouble;   940

For two thieves were returning from lying in wait for merchants.
They looked around; they saw the whiteness of her tunic.
One of them went ahead and ran to grab it.
The queen leapt up in agitation.
She thought it was a beast that wanted to eat her. 945
When this one saw that she was so pretty, he rushed to embrace her;
And the other one shouted, "Let her be, you rat!
She'll be my girl, by Saint Richier."
"Indeed, my lord, that's because she was your idea!
If you keep talking, you will pay dearly." 950
The one heard the threat; he was beside himself with anger.
He drew a big knife; he stabbed the other one with it.
The other one drew his sword; he gave him a terrible blow
So that, bleeding, they fought one another on the grass.
Queen Bertha immediately started running away; 955
And better to flee, she started to lift her skirts.
She had fled the misfortune for such a long distance, the whole length of the path,
That she was out of breath. She darted into the woods.
She went into a dense thicket to hide herself.
She did not dare to stand up again until it was dark. 960
When night came, she began to cry:
"Ah, night, how long you will be; how much I fear you.
And when it is day, so help me God,
I will not know whether to go forward or backward.
There are many reasons for me to feel distressed. 965
One of three things must come to me:
Either I shall die of hunger or cold without delay,
Or I shall be eaten before dawn.
The alternatives are poor.
Mother of God, please pray to your sweet Son 970
That he counsel me in this need,
My Lady, so truly have I great need of it."
Then she knelt; she kissed the earth.
"Saint Julien," she said, "please shelter me!"
She said her Our Father, which she did not want to delay. 975
She lay down upon her right side;
She began to make the sign of the cross of God and his Mother.
She went to sleep crying; may God protect her from danger!

XXXIX

In a very desolate place near a heath,
Beside a little hill, near a stream, 980
Slept Queen Bertha, a stone under her head.
She had commended herself to God and to good Saint Peter,
And to the Mother of God, the dear, sweet Lady,
And to Saint Julien, who was truly hospitable.
With her hands she had pulled a few ferns 985
And had covered her body and her face with them
As best she could, in front and back,
For she much feared the wind, which was cutting and fierce.
Nor did the briars leave her dress intact.
She was as young and tender as the dew on the grass. 990
She was very well-behaved and courteous and well-mannered.
She was not more than sixteen years old when the old witch
Led her out of Hungary; may she suffer a horrible death,
And may Tybert her cousin, who was false and deceiving.
May the Lady of righteousness send them great shame! 995

XL

Within the woods was the lady, who did not feel safe.
She would have been safer if she had been at Namur,
She who was related to the good Count Glansur,
Whose shield bore gold with an azure lion
And held the land of Saumur by his wife, 1000
Then was killed in battle overseas before Tyre,
Where with Saracen people he very certainly had tumultuous combat.
I do not believe that from there to Delfur was a lady
Who could have handled such a misadventure.
May the Lord God by his grace bring her good fortune, 1005
For she loved him with a very fine heart, a true and reflective one.
From pain and fatigue she slept so deeply and so hard
Beneath a small tree, next to a small, old wall,
That one could not have wakened her with the sound of a drum.

XLI

Bertha slept in the woods on the hard ground, 1010
And the night was hideous and dark.
The air was very cold,
And the lady did not have much clothing;

For she was a very young and tender creature.
But at the same time she was of so fine a nature, 1015
Of faith and belief so certain and so mature,
As one who did not concern herself with anything beyond doing good;
For she had put all her care into believing in and loving God,
So that the more the thing was difficult and heavy and hard for her
The more she took as the will of God all the evils she endured. 1020
Before midnight the weather cleared up a little,
And the moon rose beautiful and bright and pure;
And the wind was quiet and the weather calm.
It stopped raining, and the cold abated.

XLII

Right at midnight the wind stopped blowing. 1025
The queen woke up; she began to sigh.
She began to tremble with fear.
She started to look around to the right and to the left.
She thought it was day because it was so light.
"Ah, Lord God," she said, "where can I go 1030
Where I could find a little something to eat,
For I am so hungry that I hardly know what to think!"
Then the lady began to cry tenderly
And to long for her mother and her father mightily.
"Ah! My sweet mother, how much you used to love me, 1035
And you, dear, darling father, how you used to kiss me and hug me.
Never will you see me; this I can certainly promise."
On hands and knees she bent toward the earth.
"Ah! Lord God," she said, "you let yourself be nailed
To the holy cross to save your people, 1040
For which each one must serve and honor you.
The more one has to suffer, the more one must adore you;
For you can, Lord, so well recompense
Those who do. This I know without a doubt
That in your holy paradise you have them crowned. 1045
Since you allow me to suffer, dear Lord,
I want to suffer and endure hardship for you.
Now please cast me out of this danger.
For your love, here at this place I want to take
A vow that I will keep always without breaking it, 1050
That never will I say, as long as I may live,
That I am the daughter of a king nor that to noble Pépin
I am the espoused wife. Never will I seek to speak of it.

Rather I will go from door to door to ask for alms.
I will make this exception: 1055
I will tell it right away to make myself respected
So as to prevent anyone from dishonoring or shaming my body.
I want to protect my virginity, if God be willing;
For she who loses her virginity cannot recover it.
God and his Mother grant me to act in such a way with my vow 1060
That with their love I may follow the right path!"
A cloud reappeared; it began to rain.
Then she hid again in the bushes until the rain had stopped.

XLIII

Bertha, the noble one, moved along with great difficulty,
For at daybreak the weather was very cold. 1065
"Ah! God," said she, "Lord, true king, true governor,
May you protect me body and soul today;
For I have found the past night very bitter.
It has spared me no suffering.
Ah, old woman," said she, "and Tybert, evil thief, 1070
I think I am paying for your great betrayal.
May God in his pity grant that your treason will yet be discovered."
As soon as day had barely appeared in that place,
The queen departed, for the moon shone clearly.

XLIV

Through the forest of Le Mans, as soon as it was daylight, 1075
Bertha of the Big Foot went away; she stayed there no longer.
She often called upon God, the king of majesty.
She found a fountain and drank deeply from it.
Afterward she was so cold that she trembled violently.
She did not know how she could avoid the cold. 1080
The queen found a little path.
Along this path she set off; without hesitation
She pursued this path so far
That she found a hermitage; she praised God for it.
The hermitage certainly seemed to be of great antiquity. 1085
She went over and knocked at the door
With a mallet that hung attached to it;
And the hermit came there, who was full of kindness,
And unlocked a very small spy hole.
When Bertha saw the hermit, she greeted him in God's name: 1090

"Noble man," said she, "open, for holy charity,
So that I may warm myself a little,
For I am suffering and full of weariness."
When he saw her so beautiful, his heart was troubled.
He was exceedingly dazzled by her very great beauty. 1095
"God," said he, "you are my rightful protector;
Do not allow the devil to have power over me!
How did such a beautiful woman come to be in these leafy woods?
I have never seen one so beautiful in all my days.
The devil thinks he has deceived me well, 1100
But he will not have the power if God grants me strength."
He made the sign of the cross before his face; then he asked her
If she was of God; he entreated her to tell him.
"My lord," said she, "yes, I have given my heart to him."
"And say truly of whom you were born." 1105
"My lord, I am a woman full of poverty.
Let me come in; I will tell you all,
Who I am and what I seek; it will not be concealed from you."
"My beauty," the hermit said, "I have never thought
That a woman would enter here either winter or summer, 1110
For so have our superiors ordered.
Many a year has passed since this was decreed.
You shall not enter here, for thus have I vowed."
When Bertha heard this, she cried tenderly,
And the hermit gave her some of his bread. 1115
It was black and full of straw; he no longer sifted it.
Bertha took it and told him she hoped God rewarded him for this.
But she was so exhausted that she did not taste it,
She did not swallow a single morsel.
When the hermit saw that, he sighed. 1120
He could not help it; his eyes filled with tears.
She seemed to be from a good family, so he pitied her greatly.
He would have let her inside; never would he have turned her away,
But his heart was so full of faithfulness
That he feared he would falsify his vow. 1125

XLV

"My beauty," said the honorable man, "do not be angry.
Good fortune has come to you this morning;
Believe me, all will be well for you.
Prepare to go to Symon's house
And to Constance his wife, who is prudent and sensible. 1130

They are good people and wise and well thought of.
You will be well lodged there and very well warmed.
I have never seen better people, so help me God."
"My lord," Bertha said this, "I am very worried,
For I do not know the way if it is not shown to me." 1135
"My beauty," this said the hermit, "do not be afraid.
Go down this path, and do not stray from it for anything."
"My lord, may God, who made the sky and the dew, reward you for this;
For I know that I am truly dead and gone
If I have to sleep again tonight in the branchy forest, 1140
For this night I have been poorly lodged.
If I had a hundred lives, by the honored Virgin,
I would not be able to escape with one of them."
When the hermit heard her, he unlocked the door.
He put her on the path; he commended her to God. 1145
From pity he wept many a tear.
And Bertha went back into the woods, sad and tormented.
When she had traveled a part of the path,
In a big valley she met a female bear
That was running toward her with its mouth wide open. 1150
When Bertha saw it, she was terrified:
"Help, God," she said, "who made the salty sea,
Father of paradise, or my life is over!"
She fell down in a faint from fear,
And the bear left; it turned the other way. 1155
It would soon have eaten and strangled Bertha,
But God and his honored Mother protected her.
It did not please them for Bertha to go to her end in this way.
When she regained consciousness, she was so disconcerted
That she hardly knew the path. 1160
With the help of God she recognized the way again,
For she was reassured not to see the bear.
She called often upon the Mother of God.
She could not continue at all, for she was terribly tired;
For hunger and cold had so afflicted her 1165
That if God had not helped her — it is the proven truth —
She could not have lasted with such pain
Considering the way she had been brought up.
At this point Symon the forester met her.
As soon as he saw her, he drew in his rein. 1170
He felt great pity that she was so frightened.
When he saw her gray coat in which she was wrapped up
And her dress, which was ripped in many places

By briars which had torn it in the woods,
And saw Bertha so white and so flushed, 1175
He marveled greatly about who could have brought
Such a beautiful lady there.
When Bertha saw him, she stopped at once.
Symon came before her; he greeted her in the name of God.
Bertha returned his greeting, like a wise and sensible woman. 1180
"My lord, may your soul be crowned by God!
Please show me the way, if it is no trouble,
To Symon's house, which has been much praised.
You would be doing me a great service, for I am quite lost,
I have not eaten for a while; I am famished, 1185
And with the cold in these woods I have frozen this night."

XLVI

When Symon heard Bertha speak in such a manner,
She certainly seemed like a genteel lady. He took great pity upon her
So that the tears in his heart descended down his face.
"My beauty, who are you? Tell me truly." 1190
"My lord," this said the lady, "I shall tell you at once.
You should know that I was born in Alsace.
There was a great war in the country for a long time.
I am the daughter of a vavasour named Climent
Who lost his land because of it and all his domain. 1195
We were all exiled and so were all our relatives.
We seek our living in a foreign country.
I had a stepmother—may the Lord God destroy her—
Who beat me every day so painfully
With fists and feet fast and furiously 1200
That I could stand no more; I did not want to endure it further.
I left them the other day. I regret it greatly
Because since that time I have suffered great pain and great torment.
A hermit very kindly told me a little while ago
That if.I could get by chance 1205
To the home of Symon the forester, many good people are there.
I would be lodged well and gladly.
But I do not know the way there. I have been shedding many a tear about it.
Gentle, noble man, for God's sake, tell me where he is.
You would be doing me a great service, by God omnipotent." 1210
"My beauty," said Symon, "do not cry in vain.
I am the one you are looking for; you should know it truly."
When Bertha heard him, she extended her hands to God.

She could not speak for joy when she heard the worthy man.
Courteously, he led her down the path into his house. 1215
Symon called out loudly to his wife, the beautiful Constance.
She was a very worthy and intelligent woman.
"Look, sister," said he, "I have brought you a present.
I found her in these woods in marvelous fashion.
She told me her story and all her wanderings. 1220
She came from a good place; so think of that.
Last night she lay on the ground in the woods most dangerously.
I marvel greatly, by Saint Vincent,
How she escaped the beasts that way.
She is all frozen and terribly hungry. 1225
Now be very careful to help her along with her recovery."
"My lord, thus I shall be, I promise you."
She took her by the hand very courteously.
Bertha was crying from the cold and from the pain that she felt,
And Constance wept quite piteously. 1230
She led her into her room; she had her stretch out by the fire,
And know that her two beautiful daughters most humbly
Rubbed her and warmed her carefully;
And each one cried tenderly with pity.
When Bertha felt the fire, she gave thanks to God. 1235

XLVII

At Symon's house, I don't want to lie to you,
Bertha the queen was greatly pleased
That she had escaped from such evil torment.
Constance was very sad about her troubles,
And her daughters were also; each one lamented. 1240
One was named Isabelle and the other Aiglente.
They were good and beautiful and young.
Each one had gentle and gracious manners.
Each one strove to put Bertha at her ease.
They brought her food; each one presented some to her. 1245
But she had received such bad treatment in the woods
That she had more than thirty wounds.
So she could not eat, she was so weak and slow-moving.
"Ah, hermit," she said, "may God help your soul
Because you put me on the path to come here; 1250
For I was in a distressing situation
In the woods where it is cold because it rains and the wind blows."
Crying with joy, she lay face down before the fire.

XLVIII

Constance felt great pity when she saw Bertha crying
As did Symon and his daughters. Each one had a heart sincere 1255
And sweet and noble, piteous and fine and wholesome.
Each one put her hand to setting Bertha at her ease,
And Symon made the fire; he did not have an ignoble heart.
Around her they extended rugs and white straw.
They put warmed towels on her breast. 1260
"Constance," said Symon, "I really believe she is hungry."
"My lord, she will eat, by Saint Germain."
"My lady," said Bertha, "I prefer to be warmed now,
You should know that I have eaten nothing since yesterday morning.
However, the hermit gave me some of his bread; 1265
But I could not eat any. I was so exhausted."

XLIX

It was on a Monday at the beginning of the week
That Bertha was found in the forest of Maine,
Where she had suffered much hardship and pain.
But God, who is the giver of sovereign joy, 1270
Sent her on this Monday a good gift
Since she was far from her friends.
For God brings back many a lost one to the right path.
Symon went out of the room; he took all the people with him
Except for Constance and her daughters. Bertha was a member of their
    family. 1275
Each one took pains to comfort her well.
Her skin was whiter than white wool
And her hair blonder than Helen ever had.

L

Bertha was at Symon's house in the great branchy wood.
Constance and her two daughters took pity upon her. 1280
It certainly seemed and appeared
That what they did for Bertha was a valuable deed.
She ate a little bit when she was rested.
"My beauty," said Constance, "what happened to you?
How was it that you came so alone into this leafy wilderness?" 1285
Bertha soon answered her, telling her story
Just as she had recounted it to Symon.

"My beauty," Constance said, "by God the King Jesus,
You were badly advised; you realized that too late.
You lost your father because of your stepmother.   1290
You should know that you believed bad advice about the matter."
"My lady, you speak the truth. Thus I have had misfortune.
I believe that they have tried to look for me very little indeed.
For me they would not give the worth of a straw."
Through this subterfuge she kept her vow well.   1295
She never revealed the facts to the extent that she could help it.
That day Bertha warmed herself well by the fire
And ate and drank at her pleasure.

LI

"My beauty," said Constance, "do not be troubled.
What is your name? You are welcome here."   1300
"My lady, my name is Bertha; may God help me."
"That is a fortunate name; this name becomes you.
That is the name of King Pépin's fiancée,
The daughter of the king of Hungary; there is none better on earth.
Everyone says there is no more beautiful girl to be seen."   1305
When Bertha heard this, she became upset.
It troubled her that her name was not unknown.
"My beauty," Constance said, "you have been miserable.
How long have you been lost in the woods?"
"My lady, since yesterday morning; and I am distressed.   1310
I was in the woods during the night and slept all alone.
I found many a briar and many a sharp thorn
Which have torn up my dress and destroyed it entirely.
They have made many a mark on my bare skin,
For I fled with fear like a frightened animal.   1315
May God return to you the love you have shown me.
God and his Mother helped me so much today
When I came out of the forest so early in the morning.
You have warmed me up again well and have nourished me very well.
I had great need of it; I was completely overcome."   1320

LII

Bertha greatly regretted that she had told them her name.
She would have much preferred that she had lied to them.
"Constance," said Symon, "make her up a bed
So that she can rest and sleep a little;

For in the woods last night she had little comfort." 1325
"My lord," said Bertha, "may God repay you!
Now I cannot say that the good, honest hermit
Who saw me this morning so early and taught me the way
Held me in contempt; may God have mercy on his soul!
If he had not, I would have been dead; that cannot be denied." 1330
Then she said under her breath so that no one could hear her,
"This God who was born of the Virgin in Bethlehem,
May he destroy Tybert, the evil one, the deceiver,
And Margiste, the old woman who has thus betrayed me!
My father, the king with the brave heart, would not believe, 1335
Nor Blanchefleur my mother, nor my sister Aelis
That giving me a husband would put me in such a situation.
I know well that if they knew it, many a heart would be distressed
In their kingdom and would be sad and afflicted."
Then she began to cry; her heart was troubled. 1340

LIII

"Bertha," said Constance, "do not be discouraged.
Your stepmother has beaten and mistreated you.
Know that what she has done is evil and despicable.
God will repay her, you may be sure, all she deserves.
A bad stepmother has very little love. 1345
Let all of this go; let not a word be said of it;
For in this house you will not be subjected to such treatment.
I will let you stay here for a whole month.
Anything you ask for will be given you."
"My lady," said Bertha, "I shall not refuse this gift! 1350
May God reward you and the honest hermit!
May your soul and his be blessed this day
By the Father and the Son and the Holy Spirit!"

LIV

In the beautiful forest where there are many tall fir trees,
In the house of Symon and Constance of the gentle heart 1355
Was Bertha the queen. She bowed her head frequently.
Very often she prayed that God would send a good end
To the one who had put her on the path to this place.
Constance of the sincere heart gave her much thought
And so did her two daughters. May God give them a good destiny! 1360
One brought her a young chicken to eat,

And the other refilled her drink with fresh wine.
Then they covered her warmly with gray fur and ermine.
Their hearts were much distressed about her from evening till morning.
God, how did Constance not deduce now that she was Pépin's wife? 1365

LV

In Symon's house, in the stone chamber,
Lay Bertha of the Big Foot under a bed-curtain.
God, how could Constance have not guessed that it was the queen
That they had left in the wilderness?
If she had known it, she would have been very deferential 1370
Now that she was so close to her.
Bertha made herself loved like one who ceaselessly helps out others
The way a poor maiden does
Because she was thoughtful and good and prudent and well-mannered.
She would not have broken her vow even if she had been whipped. 1375
She would rather have had her heart pulled out of her chest
Like one who was full of very sincere faith.
Constance showed her that she did not hate her.
Indeed, she loved her more than her daughters for her good behavior.

LVI

The two daughters of Constance, I will not lie to you, 1380
Knew how to work gold and silk; for I know it well.
Near them sat Bertha, whose heart was true.
When she saw their work, she said, "I'll show you something
That I shall teach you if you wish.
My mother was an embroiderer, born near Alsace." 1385
"Bertha," said Isabelle, "I will be obliged if you would teach me."
Then Bertha started working, as I shall tell you,
Just as I found it in the book at Saint Denis.
There was not a better embroiderer from Tours to Cambrai.
"Isabelle," said Aiglente, "I shall not hide it from you. 1390
What we know about this amounts to a blade of grass.
I shall go straight to my mother; I shall tell her
That if Bertha leaves us, I shall never be happy."
She went running to her mother; she did not wait long.
"My lady, by the faith that I owe to God and Saint Nicholas, 1395
Bertha is the best embroiderer that I have ever seen.
You should know that if she leaves, I shall go with her.
I shall not leave my sister Isabelle."

"Be quiet, dear daughter; I shall keep her with me.
If she wants to stay, I shall never fail in my responsibilities to her.   1400
And if she deserves it, I shall find her a husband.
I shall put you and her together as companions.
You two will sleep together in my room."
Aiglente of the gentle and true heart laughed with joy.
"Dear Mother," she said, "I shall thank God for it   1405
When I have such a companion with me;
For never before have I seen or been acquainted with such a sweet thing.
She is more gracious than the rose in May."

LVII

Constance went into the room; she did not delay any longer,
And Aiglente her daughter, who was very joyous and merry, went in also.   1410
They found Bertha embroidering very fine and excellent work.
To embroider well and correctly gave her very little trouble.
When Constance saw it, her heart rejoiced.
"Bertha," Constance said, "there is nothing that I have that
Is not at your command; everything I have is yours.   1415
Be completely a part of my household,
And may I be shamed if I do not pay you well."
"My lady, may God by whom the sun rises reward you.
I shall serve you very well, however hard it is for me."

LVIII

"My lady, I shall stay with you, since it pleases you.   1420
May the true God who never lies reward you.
May the hour be blessed that I first saw you."
Bertha made herself beloved by all; I tell you as much;
But we shall leave off speaking of her here;
And when the time comes, we shall return to her.   1425
She was with Constance fully nine and a half years
And with Symon, whom she found a good friend.
She did so much that no one in the household was her superior.
She carried all the keys, which she had deserved to do.
On Saturdays she lived only on bread and water,   1430
And on Fridays she wore a hair shirt
In honor of Jesus, who pardoned Longinus,
And of his sweet Mother from whom he came and was born.
She prayed for King Pépin; she did not forget him,
That God protect him and finally have mercy upon his soul.   1435

King Flore her father she regretted much also
And Blanchefleur her mother, who had reared her so gently.
"Ah, Mother," said she, "how your heart would be distressed
If you knew how the servant betrayed me!
You married me to a rich husband, 1440
For I am married to God, who does not lie.
He is the sovereign king to whom I have entrusted myself.
May he protect you, I pray with all my heart,
And the good king my father, the bold knight."

LIX

Here we shall leave Bertha, may Jesus bless her, 1445
Who has taken lodging with Constance
In Symon's house in the ancient forest.
They were extremely good people and of very saintly life.
Before she had spent half a year there
She was so beloved in this home, 1450
And Symon and Constance and their entire household
And their children, indeed, everyone grew to cherish her so
That they loved her with all their hearts, as people with proper upbringing do.
Symon made her his niece and Constance her friend.
Each one brought her honor, sweetness, and company. 1455
We shall speak to you of Pépin of the bold face
And of the evil old woman who betrayed her lady
And of Aliste her daughter; may God curse her.
Right after Bertha was taken from Paris
And carried off into the great forest 1460
Where Tybert and the others left her,
The king was at Paris, the sovereign city.
He truly believed, don't doubt it at all,
That it was his wife with him in his domain
And that the servant was the daughter of the king of Hungary. 1465
While Bertha was separated from Pépin,
He had two children by the hated servant.
One was named Rainfrois: he was full of deceit;
And the other Heudris: he was false and full of greed.
May the Lord God, the Son of holy Mary, destroy them. 1470
For afterward many fine people were destroyed by them
And many a betrayal planned and pursued
As you will hear if someone tells you.
This servant had so dishonored the land of France
By the advice of her mother, the filthy, wrinkled old woman, 1475

That she had established many a bad custom.
She imposed taxes and tolls on the country by act of authority
By which the poor people were very badly governed,
And the land in many places was much impoverished.
In lovely Paris, people still maintain 1480
That the city was much more in subjection
Than it was before; afterward it was not set aright.
Indeed, most of the time in the past
One could not undo something even when one had sworn to.
There was not a priory or an abbey in the country 1485
To which the servant had not done outrageous things.
There were none so bold as to contradict her,
For they much feared her very great wickedness.
The more outrage and deviltry the servant committed
The more her mother was merry and joyous and happy. 1490

LX

You have surely heard that Rainfrois was the name
Of the very first child that the king and the servant had.
The other was named Heudris; they were wicked and treacherous.
They sent messengers to Hungary twice,
To King Flore, who was sensible and courteous, 1495
To Blanchefleur his wife, who had blond hair.
They gave the messengers horses and palfreys.
They had their choice of possessions and great riches.
They made arrangements to return right away.
They came back to France with very rich baggage. 1500
If King Flore had known that his daughter was in the woods
And what her situation was, he would not have been joyous.
His daughter the duchess and his son Godefrois
Died together—I know that truly—
Fourteen months after the marriage of Bertha. 1505
King Flore was sad as was reasonable and right.
One daughter remained to him; she was the heir of Saxony.
Then a Saracen king took Saxony from her,
Towns and castles and cities, forts and domains
Because his ancestors had held it formerly. 1510
Justamont was his name; he was master of their laws.
After him was Guithechin, who never liked the French.
This one was the son of Justamont; he was very arrogant;
For he believed he could conquer France and Orleans,
Knights of Champagne and Burgundy and knights of Flanders and England. 1515

He went as far as Cologne; there he caused much turmoil.
He held Saxony a long time, for no one ever defended it;
But then it was reconquered by the French and the Germans.
At the reconquering were the baron Hurupois
And knights from Flanders, Brabant, and the Ardennes. 1520
But henceforth you will no longer hear of this matter.
I shall now return to the first story.

LXI

King Flore was sad, for it weighed heavily upon him
That his daughter the duchess was dead
And Godefrois his son, who held the tower of Argoise. 1525
He had no more heirs except for Bertha, the courteous;
May the Lord God counsel her wherever she may go.
I shall come back to our French people,
Who saw plainly that the servant was defrauding them
And that she was taking their goods and their riches by force. 1530
She even took a tenth of the woodcutting.
Never did anyone say a word about it nor make any protest.
No one dared to speak of it; everyone kept quiet.

LXII

The servant made herself terribly feared and dreaded.
She did so much that she was vehemently hated everywhere. 1535
She imposed taxes on the merchants;
And when anyone spoke of it—this is no lie—
She had Tybert make the men at arms seize him
And then made him lie in prison so long
That when he could leave he was very happy. 1540
Each one feared that he would fall into their hands.
They preferred to give what they had than to die
Or to be made to languish in prison.
They accumulated a great deal of wealth, may God curse them,
For the king let them do exactly as they wished; 1545
For in the servant he had put heart and body and desire.
Whoever looked at her well and at leisure
Certainly would say that you could not find a more beautiful woman.
But she was so wicked that she never obeyed God
And neither wanted to go to church nor come from it. 1550
Ever since they tried to have their lady murdered
And first had the intention to betray her

Between her and her mother, may God bring disgrace upon them,
And had Tybert agree with them to do it,
They could not hear a mass all the way through; 1555
For, you understand, God would not allow it.
God lets many people accomplish treason
But in the end God knows how to punish them.
Their treason appears before they die.
For many a time God makes right come back to right. 1560

LXII

The evil servant imposed so much, may God make her suffer,
In the kingdom of France, by force and by power,
On everything that she could find to tax,
On pepper, on cumin, on spices, on wax
And on wheat and on wine; she had everything written together. 1565
I would not know how to specify it all item by item.
She assembled so much wealth that I would not know how to describe it,
For which many poor people felt sorrow and anger.
Her treasure often made her laugh with joy;
But if she had been prudent, she ought to have despaired, 1570
For in the end she got the worst of it.

LXIV

In France the servant assembled great riches.
She took everything everywhere, wherever she could have it.
She made the heart of many a poor and many a rich person sorrow.
She had a strong desire to accomplish her will. 1575
She had put all her hope in assembling treasure,
But she had neglected faith and loyalty.
She imposed so many evil institutions on the kingdom
That those who are there now are affected by them.
One day King Flore was in one of his great manors 1580
In Hungary on a Sunday evening.
Near him was Blanchefleur, whose heart was sad and somber
For her daughter Bertha whom she desired to see.
"My lady," said King Flore, "now we have no heir
Except Bertha, who often makes my heart grieve, 1585
Who has gone to live so far from us.
I would like very much to have little Heudriet
So that we could give him our land and all our possessions.
If almighty God wished him to live,

He would be king of Hungary; nothing could stop it.   1590
We shall send to France to know if this can work.
Pépin would surely want it to be as I hope."
"This idea," said the lady, "pleases me and that is what I would like."

LXV

One Tuesday morning, the story states,
Blanchefleur and King Flore sent to France   1595
A certain messenger who was entirely credible.
He did not have to be instructed about how to take a message properly.
He was not like those who drink too much
So that they lose the sense and memory of it
And do not know how to convey a truthful word of it.   1600
He prepared his baggage well and soon and properly
And was very well mounted on a black mule.
No trip was too great for him to complete.
He went right to France, you may be sure.
He found King Pépin at Tours, which sits on the Loire.   1605

LXVI

When the messenger had made his preparations,
He went to King Pépin; he did not tarry.
Graciously and courteously he greeted the king
And gave him the letter on behalf of King Flore.
The king opened the wax; he saw within   1610
That Flore and Blanchefleur, too, had asked for
One of his children out of great friendship.
And he found in the letter that they had decided
That he would be king of Hungary, and he read of their anguish
And that they would never have any heir—it is the very truth—   1615
And that they were all dead and gone to their end
Except for Bertha, who was so beautiful.
When Pépin heard it, he felt great pity.
Then he sat down to eat as soon as he had washed,
And our French led the messenger from him   1620
To the false queen; may God curse her.
So he gave his message as he had been ordered.
He brought her the letters as he had been commanded.
The servant expressed great joy over it; she honored him greatly.
When she had read the letter and had seen in it   1625
That no child was left to King Flore

Except Bertha the queen, whom they held very dear,
By deceitfulness she wept a little tear,
And Margiste her mother sighed greatly over it
Like one who was full of falsity   1630
And great treachery and disloyalty.
May the Lord God, the king of majesty, bring her harm!
When the messenger had spoken enough to the lady,
They led him before the king, and he dined.
Until the next day he stayed at Tours.   1635

LXVII

Early the next morning, right after sunrise,
The messenger got up; he did not want to delay.
He heard the mass at Saint Martin's church.
He took his leave of the servant when she had gotten up.
He commended the servant and Margiste to God.   1640
They gave him letters sealed in wax.
He left the servant sad and tearful, so it appeared.
Then he came before Pépin in the paved hall.
When the king saw him, he told him his intention thus:
"Friend, you are going away to your country.   1645
Give King Flore my greetings, God willing,
And my lady Blanchefleur, the wise queen.
Their affliction weighs upon me, by the honored Virgin.
But so things come in accordance with God's will and pleasure.
Of Heudriet my son say that for no one   1650
Would his mother be deprived of him a single day."
The messenger understood well that the thing was decided
And that King Flore's hopes were in vain.
He took his leave and went away; he hastened so upon his way
That he arrived in Hungary with scarcely a stop.   1655
He told the king the news in every detail,
That Pépin's child would not be guardian of his land.
It must be peopled by another lineage.
When the king heard it, he was much displeased,
And Blanchefleur was greatly saddened.   1660
She was so distressed and so greatly tormented
That she nearly fainted with grief.
Even the people of the kingdom were much disturbed.

LXVIII

You have certainly heard it said and told many a time
That treason and murder will out. 1665
The evil servant behaved with great falseness
Who brought much pain to her rightful lady.
God did not want her to suffer any more, for it did not please him
Who of all misdeeds is Lord and judge.
The good person who can should guard himself from doing evil. 1670
God lets many people do their treason,
But then he makes them reveal their misdeeds so
That all their wrongdoing turns back upon themselves,
And one can clearly recognize what they have done.

LXIX

Blanchefleur the queen was of very high birth 1675
And believed deeply in God and had a good heart.
One night she was lying near the wise Flore
In the land of Hungary in one of their handsome houses.
As she was sleeping, it seemed to her that a savage bear
Was eating her right arm, side, and buttock 1680
And that an eagle had come to sit on her face.
She was afraid, so she woke up; she was shaken to the core.
She was so frightened that nothing could assuage her fear.
Her heart was so grieved that she nearly went insane.

LXX

Blanchefleur woke up with her heart greatly distressed. 1685
She told the king her dream; he interpreted it favorably.
"My lord," said the queen, "for the sake of God who does not lie,
Give me a gift, I beg of you out of love.
Let me go to France this Easter
To see Bertha my daughter, the darling one that I love so, 1690
Or my heart will break in two."
"My lady," said the king, "by Saint Remi,
How could we be apart for so long?"
"My lord," said the lady, "for the love of God, have mercy!
Has it not already been nearly eight and a half years 1695
Since Bertha our daughter has seen us, or we her?
We show poorly how much we love her."
When the king heard her, he was a little sad.

The lady begged him so much that he agreed
For her to go, but on condition that 1700
She bring back, if she could, either Rainfrois or Heudris.
"My lord, I will do it; I pledge you my faith
That I shall bring back either Rainfrois or Heudris."
"My lady," said the king, "I give you permission to go."

LXXI

The queen felt great joy when the king gave her his permission 1705
To go to France, the beautiful.
"My lady," said the king, "do you know what I ask of you?
Since you insist on going to France,
I want noble knights to go with you.
You will take one hundred knights in your company 1710
Of the most valiant ones in all Hungary.
I do not want you to go with a small entourage,
For the French people do not hesitate to display their wealth."
When the lady heard it, she was very joyous and glad.
As she was well-mannered and courteous, she thanked her husband for it. 1715
She prepared her baggage without delay.
Just as the king had told her,
Blanchefleur equipped it as one who is well brought up.
She left one clear dawn.
The king accompanied her a good day and a half. 1720
Upon taking his leave, the king kissed her most sweetly.
He commended her to God, the Son of holy Mary.
And so he went back. Before she saw him again, she would be greatly disturbed
And troubled at heart and quite angry.
They crossed many a land, many an ancient forest, 1725
And many a great river which carries ships well
Until they came into France, the sovereign land.
When the people of the kingdom heard the news,
That she was the mother of the queen, none failed to curse her;
They often prayed that God would give her such sickness 1730
That before she returned she would be dead and buried
And that her soul would be carried away into hell.
"When you endure such a queen as torments us this way
And she abuses you as she does by her evil life,
Curse her mother's soul!" 1735
The news was announced to Blanchefleur

That her daughter was hated like this in the kingdom.
When she heard the news, she was very sad.
Her heart was much aggrieved and disconcerted.
"God," she said, "where is such deviltry coming from? 1740
Bertha my daughter was brought up in such a good place
And was born and came from such a good family
From her father and her mother and from old ancestry.
Where is this bad disposition now coming from
That she steals from the people by trickery? 1745
There is no more valiant man from here to Syria
Than is Flore her father, nor one more without villainy.
I myself do not like outrage or foolishness.
Thus I am so distressed that I do not know what to say.
Before I return, I will so have chastised her 1750
That I will make her give back all that she has seized
Because of which the poor people are in poverty and badly governed.
I am not at all satisfied with this news."

LXXII

Then Blanchefleur, whose heart was sincere, went away.
She was much annoyed with her daughter Bertha, 1755
Of whom the people everywhere complained without reserve.
In the middle of the road she met a rude peasant.
When he saw Blanchefleur, he took hold of her bridle.
"My lady, for the mercy of God, I am complaining about your daughter.
I had only one horse by which I earned my bread, 1760
By which I kept myself and my wife Margain
And my little children, who now will die of hunger.
With the horse I carried thatch and logs and straw to Paris.
It cost me sixty sous a year ago, for certain.
Now she has had it taken away from me; may God give her a bad tomorrow! 1765
It caused me hardship to feed it this winter.
But, by the holy Lord who made Eve from Adam,
I will curse her so, from evening till morning,
That I will have vengeance for it from the sovereign Father."
The lady had pity on him; her heart was filled with sadness. 1770
She had one hundred sous placed in his hand at once.
He kissed the stirrup and the harness:
"My lady, may God reward you, for now my heart is happy and whole.
Never will I curse Bertha, by Saint Germain."

LXXIII

It was on a Monday, at the beginning of the week, 1775
That Blanchefleur, the beauty, may God bless her,
Went toward Paris, which sits on the Seine.
She was dressed in rich clothing, which was dyed scarlet.
She heard news of her daughter that made her heart heavy.
Everyone complained of her; within her heart she grieved greatly. 1780
"Ha! Lord God," said she, "who sat at the Last Supper,
Noble Mother of God, sovereign queen,
How does it happen that my daughter, who is more beautiful than Helen,
Makes herself hated this way by people near and far?
When she left my country, she was full of all goodness. 1785
There was not a more refined person from there to the ports of Aquitaine.
Now she has certainly muddied her clear fountain,
For she is the most hated that ever wore wool clothing.
God, by thy great sweetness, lead her back to the right way!"

LXXIV

Then the queen went away toward the city of Paris. 1790
To King Pépin a message was sent
That Blanchefleur had entered his country.
When the king heard it, he was very pleased.
He himself went to tell it, I believe,
Into the room of the servant of the fair face. 1795
When she heard it, her heart was very distressed.
She acted as if she were happy and let out a false laugh.
King Pépin left at once,
And the servant remained; her heart was very heavy.
She called her mother immediately—she did not delay long— 1800
And Tybert her cousin; may God curse him.
In the room all three sat down on the rug.
"Mother," said the servant, "by Saint Denis,
Blanchefleur the queen is already in Cambresis.
I do not know what we can do; the situation could not be worse." 1805
When Tybert heard it, he was greatly troubled.
"Tybert," the old woman said, "don't be so distressed.
I can propose a stratagem:
My daughter will pretend to be sick the whole time
And unable to get out of bed for anything. 1810
If we can stop them before they get here,
These people who are coming, by the God of paradise,

Then there will not be any concern about this; by faith, I promise you."
"My lady," said Tybert, "may you be blessed!
When necessity arises, we can count on your intelligence and judgment! 1815
Without you we would not know anything."
It was established that they would keep to this plan,
And then they very soon prepared the bed
And the servant lay down; may she be shamed!

LXXV

Then the evil servant was put into her bed. 1820
She made great pretense of being ill; she was full of deception.
The old woman trembled with fear under her tunic.
May the Lord God and Saint Denis destroy her!
"Ha! God," said the old woman, "true king full of nobility,
What devils have taught Blanchefleur the way here? 1825
Damn whoever told her to come
When my daughter's heart is so sad and undone because of it!"
To comfort her daughter she sat down near her,
For she was so afraid that she felt she was about to break into pieces.
"Daughter," the old woman said, "do you know what I'm thinking? 1830
A Jewess once taught me how to poison.
I know how to do it better than any woman from here to Friesland.
I shall betray Blanchefleur with a pear or a cherry.
I shall soon find and procure some poison."
When the servant heard it, she did not think well of this counsel. 1835

LXXVI

"Mother," said the servant, "this advice is not good.
I want to get up from here and get ready.
I think it is best that we flee.
I know very well that I shall be recognized by my feet.
I do not have half of such feet or such heels 1840
As had Bertha, our lady that we have betrayed.
It was by your advice, which was a great mistake.
I advise in good faith that now we should go away.
We will put plates of silver and gold on the pack horses.
We'll leave my two children here with their father. 1845
They have not deserved death; let's not even think about it.
In the middle of the night we'll get on the road.
Let's go to Puglia or Calabria or Sicily.
And we shall take our cousin Tybert with us,

For he has well merited that we not fail him. 1850
Lending at usury will keep us very well.
Otherwise, I do not see how we can escape;
For if they find out all our evil deeds, I know very well that we shall we burned."
"By God," said the old woman, "we shall not flee.
Let me arrange things; we shall manage so well 1855
That we shall poison King Pépin, too.
Until we bring this to a good end
We shall use batting gauze to block out the light entirely from the doors and windows.
Lie completely still, for we shall so well deceive
That neither your eyes, your nose, nor your chin will be seen. 1860
In this manner we shall extricate ourselves easily."
"Mother," said the servant, "we shall follow your advice.
May God and his holy names advise us
That from this thing we may well escape;
For if we can do this task in this way, 1865
We shall have managed wisely and well."

LXXVII

They kept to this decision. The old woman got up.
She arranged it all in the way they had planned.
Immediately the doors and windows were all blocked.
She left Tybert the traitor to guard the door. 1870
She went before King Pépin all in tears.
When she saw the king, she called him aside.
King Pépin saw very well that she was crying.
"What's the matter?" said the king. "Don't keep it from me."
"My lord," said the old woman, "things are going badly for me. 1875
Madame the queen has just gone to bed
So ill that she can scarcely get up.
It has just now come upon her; I do not know what is the matter with her.
I do not believe that Blanchefleur will ever come in time."
When the king heard it, he was greatly disturbed. 1880
The old woman made a great display of grief; then she went back.
She went to her daughter; she gave her much comfort
And told her how she had spoken to King Pépin.
The news went through the whole city
That the lady was sick and that she would die. 1885
When the people heard it, each one was glad.
They cursed in the name of God, creator of all things, the person
Who would give any advice towards curing her.
"May God curse the one who brought her to us

And who first introduced her to the French people 1890
And who first gave her to King Pépin;
And may he destroy the mother who carried her in her womb,
And cursed be the father who ever engendered her;
For never did a more untrustworthy woman ever live."
So I will stop talking about her, but I will come back to this soon. 1895
A messenger appeared who greeted the king
And who announced news of Blanchefleur.
He told him that she would hear mass at Montmartre.
When the king heard it, he got on his horse at once;
And Rainfrois and Heudris both went with him. 1900
Many a highly-placed person rode beside the children;
Archbishop and bishop, each got themselves ready,
And duke and count and prince; none stayed behind.
They went to meet Blanchefleur, who would be much distressed
Once she learned the news of Bertha, her daughter. 1905

LXXVIII

King Pépin of France was very much dismayed,
For with the queen's illness he thought he had lost everything.
From there to Montmartre they did not stop.
They found the queen, and the entourage greeted her,
And Blanchefleur graciously returned their greeting. 1910
She embraced the king kindly.
Then she asked him—she did not wait any longer—
"How is it going with my daughter Bertha, for the sake of Jesus, the true king?"
"My lady, I shall tell you. As soon as she knew
That you were coming to see her, she was so joyous, 1915
Her heart was so open and so moved with joy
That she has never gotten up; she has never left her bed.
But she will recover when she has seen you."
When Blanchefleur heard this, she was deeply troubled;
She thought it was her daughter that she had news of. 1920

LXXIX

Sorrowful was the lady; she was silent and speechless,
For she had not had any news that did not turn into bad tidings.
King Pépin took her by her bare white hand.
"My lady," said the king, "do not be downcast.
Be cheerful; your arrival is fortunate, 1925
For your daughter will be cured when you have seen her

And sweetly taken her lovingly in your arms."
And behold! Here were the king's sons riding along the street.
Then they dismounted to walk under a leafy overhang.
Each of them courteously greeted the queen. 1930
"My lady," said the king, "you should be proud.
These two are my children by your daughter, my darling wife."
When Blanchefleur saw them, her blood ran cold.
Her heart did not quicken with joy.
She greeted them without warmth; she broke out in a cold sweat. 1935

LXXX

Blanchefleur the queen, who was very kind,
Looked at the children, who were young.
She did not kiss them or hug them at all
Because her heart did not prompt her to; you should know this is the truth.
And the people who were there were not pleased with her. 1940
They secretly nudged one another
And talked among themselves
And said that she acted that way out of very great meanness.
"You can understand why her daughter is so unfriendly.
There's not another woman in all the world with as much falsity. 1945
Cursed be the first who brought her to the kingdom!
She is lying very sick; may one hundred thousand devils
Grant that she die tonight."
They came out of the church; they did not stay there any longer.
The king and his noblemen were dressed in dark fabric. 1950
Many a duke, many a count was there; many a bishop, many an abbot.
The queen's people put her on her horse; then the king's people mounted.
King Pépin was on the right; then they turned away from there.
She was often cursed—I won't hide it from you—
For love of the servant; may God grant her misfortune. 1955
Blanchefleur's heart was sad and angry.
She knew very well that if her daughter were in good health
She would have seen her or sent her some message.
They went down to Paris, the admirable city.
She looked at the country far and wide. 1960
It pleased her greatly once she had cast her gaze upon it.

LXXXI

The lady was at Montmartre; she looked at the valley.
She saw the city of Paris, which is both long and wide:

Many a tower, many a hall, and many a chimney.
She saw the great, crenellated tower of Montlhéry.
She saw the river Seine, which was very wide,
With many vines planted on each side.
She saw Pontoise and Poissy and Meulans in the plain,
Marly, Montmorency, and Conflans in the meadow,
Dammartin-en-Goële, which was well protected,
And many other large towns which I have not named.
The land and all the countryside pleased her very much.
"Ah, God," she said, "Lord who made the sky and the dew,
How richly my daughter Bertha married;
And she came to and arrived at a very noble place."
King Pépin, riding along on her right, honored her greatly
And often asked news of King Flore.
"My lord," said the queen, who was wise and sensible,
"He is hale and hearty, thank God.
If he knew I had found his daughter here
In such a disordered state of health,
His joy would very quickly turn to great sorrow;
For he loves his daughter more than anything in this world."
"My lady," said Pépin, "do not worry about that;
For, God willing, she will soon be completely recovered.
When she sees you, her illness will be gone;
For her joy will be one hundred doubles doubled."
She entered the city, which was very well decorated.
At the windows appeared many a lady dressed in finery.
The whole main thoroughfare was entirely draped with curtains.
All eyes turned to Blanchefleur.
For love of the servant she received this day
Many a wretched curse, uttered in a low voice and concealed.
She dismounted at the stairway of the paved hall.
The king and the noblemen led her to the palace;
And there was Margiste, who had cried copiously.
She had scratched herself a bit with her fingernails.
She came before Blanchefleur as if demented.
She let herself fall at her feet as if she had fainted.
Blanchefleur recognized her, and she raised her up.
She kissed her; crying, she hugged her hard.
"Margiste, where is my daughter? Have her shown to me!"
"My lady," Margiste said, "woe that I was ever born
When you have found your daughter in such a state!
Since she heard news of you
She has not been well, evening or morning.

Her joy was so extreme
Because she has yearned for you for such a long time
That never since has she budged from her bed.
Let her rest until twilight." 2010
When Blanchefleur heard it, she was greatly frightened.
She went out of the hall and into the bedroom.
Her heart was heavy with sorrow; she was extremely worried.
The old woman returned at once
To the servant in her bedroom, which was quite well sealed from the light, 2015
Very well curtained off with gold and silk drapery.

LXXXII

Blanchefleur the queen had a deeply sorrowful heart,
And the king comforted her with much kindness.
"My lord," said Blanchefleur, "by Saint Vincent,
When I left King Flore, I promised him 2020
That I would persuade you to agree
To make him a present of one of your children.
If our daughter does not recover,
We will make him king; you should know it."
"My lady," said Pépin, "do whatever your heart desires and don't worry about it, 2025
And I will gladly do all you ask."
"My lord," said the queen, "I thank you from the bottom of my heart."
The tables were set without long delay.
Four hundred knights sat down to eat.
The king greatly honored Blanchefleur and her people. 2030
After dinner, Blanchefleur did not wait any longer.
She went quickly to where she thought her daughter was.
The old woman came; she hugged her.
"My lady," said the old woman, "by Saint Clement,
I told the queen that you would not come at all 2035
Before it is close to evening.
She has gone to sleep for a little while; go back, for God's sake!"
"Gladly," said the lady, who meant no harm;
"I will stay right here, by God omnipotent.
I will not leave here, you should know, 2040
Until I have seen my daughter Bertha, the fair,
And kissed her mouth, God willing, gently."
When the old woman heard it, she was displeased.
She was so afraid that her heart nearly broke in two.
May God who made the earth destroy her! 2045

LXXXIII

In a very beautiful little grassy courtyard beneath a leafy branch
Right in front of the bedroom of the filthy, stinking servant,
Sat Blanchefleur, who was going insane with grief.
She was very anxious and sorrowful for her daughter.
God! If only the lady had known the misery and torment   2050
That her daughter Bertha, the noble beauty, had suffered
Because of the evil old woman — may God destroy her —
And by Tybert also, who put great effort into
Comforting the servant, who was scared out of her wits.
May God send all three of them such a fierce attack   2055
That from their false bargain they come to their just deserts!

LXXXIV

Blanchefleur was seated under a branch in a grassy little courtyard.
She called the false old woman — may fire burn her muzzle —
And she came right away.
"Tell me," said the lady, "by Saint Marcel,   2060
Who or what made my daughter engage in such deeds of trickery
That everyone young and old complains of her?
Now you should know truly that this is not something I condone,
For in a hated lady there is much evil pleasure."
"My lady, they are wrong, by God who made Daniel.   2065
Cursed be the hide of whoever told you this;
For never a better lady had a ring on her finger,
For she has been doing all this only for entertainment."

LXXXV

Blanchefleur the queen had no desire to rejoice.
She remembered other things to talk to the old woman about.   2070
"Where is your daughter Aliste now?"
"My lady, I will tell you. You should know truly that
She died suddenly going to the toilet.
I do not know what disease afflicted her under her right jaw.
I really believe in the end it must have been leprosy.   2075
You should know that the heart under my breast hurt me so over it,
For she was very skillful and pleasant and quick.
I had her buried near an old chapel

Secretly so that people did not know about it."
Thus the old woman told the lie, 2080
But the affair would not go on much longer.

LXXXVI

Blanchefleur was at that spot for two days, that's no lie,
So that she could not get to the servant.
For Tybert and the old woman, may God curse them,
Always took turns to better guard the door. 2085
A little before supper, just about twilight,
Blanchefleur took a desire—she did not want to suffer any more—
To see her daughter; she could not restrain herself.
Against his will, she made Tybert open the door.
A young maid, may God bless her, 2090
Who was almost a noblewoman—the king had had her brought up—
Lit a candle, for one could not see in there.
But the old woman struck her with a stick
So hard that she made the blood flow to the ground.
"Go away, filthy strumpet! Madame wants to sleep. 2095
She cannot see any light for anything."
When the maid was treated this way, she began to tremble
Violently and started to flee.
She saw very well that the old woman was full of evil spirit.
Blanchefleur was distressed by this, but she wanted so much 2100
To go to her daughter that she made no objection.
She came to the servant's bed, so she began to feel it.
"Mother, welcome," said the servant
So feebly that the lady could scarcely hear it.
"My lady, how is my father? May God bless him." 2105
"Daughter, he was doing well when I had to part from him."
"My lady, Jesus be praised.
I am not able now to entertain you,
And that distresses me so much that I think I'll die
That I cannot rejoice with you as I would like." 2110

LXXXVII

The servant was more frightened than I can tell you.
Her whole body trembled; she did not feel like laughing.
Beneath Blanchefleur's gaze she tossed and turned constantly.
"Daughter," said Blanchefleur, "my whole heart is torn apart
By not seeing you, for I desire to greatly." 2115

"Mother," said the servant, "I am suffering such torment
That I have become as yellow as wax.
The doctors tell me that light makes me worse
And talking also; nothing is worse for me.
I dare not see you; my heart is in great anguish from that. 2120
My heart draws me so to the king my father
That I do not know what to do; I am about to go to pieces.
Let me rest; may Jesus reward you for it."

LXXXVIII

When Blanchefleur heard the servant speak this way,
She saw clearly that she wanted her to leave. 2125
She felt the grief she had from it deep in her heart.
"Help, God," said she, "who never lied!
This is not my daughter that I have found here.
If she had been half dead, by Saint Remi,
She would have kissed me many times and given me a good welcome." 2130
In anger she got up; she waited no longer.
She half opened the big door of the room.
She called her attendants, who were waiting for her there.
"Come here," she said, "for God's sake, I pray you.
I did not find my daughter," she said. "They have lied to me about everything. 2135
I will know if God has allowed this to take place."
Tybert, who was guarding the door, reddened with fear.
Blanchefleur the queen did not delay long there.
She went back into the chamber, and her attendants did, too.
They pulled down on the floor many a golden curtain, many a rug. 2140
"My lady," said the old woman, "for the love of God, have mercy!
Do you want to kill your daughter? She hasn't slept for three days."
"Hold your tongue, old woman," she said. "I will not do anything for you."
They opened the windows; they did not slow down.
When Tybert and the servant saw how it was going, 2145
Now don't ask at all if they were scared to death.
Blanchefleur came to the bed where she saw the servant.
She seized all the covers with her two hands.
She pulled them so that she uncovered the servant completely.
Blanchefleur saw the feet; her heart failed her entirely. 2150
The servant took a sheet; she jumped down out of the bed.
Blanchefleur threw her down to the floor by her hair,
Which was very blond, I declare.
Everyone came into the chamber when they heard the cry.
They took her out of Blanchefleur's hands, and she fled 2155

Into another chamber where her people received her.
And Blanchefleur cried, "Help! Betrayed! Betrayed!
She is not my daughter at all! Alas! Sorrow! Oh, woe is me!
It is Margiste's daughter that I have raised with me.
They have murdered my child Bertha, who loved me so." 2160
A messenger went to the king and reported it all to him,
And Pépin ran there when he heard the news,
And many another nobleman followed him closely.
When they heard the news, they were all astonished.

LXXXIX

Blanchefleur the queen was nearly out of her mind. 2165
When she saw Pépin, she screamed at him, weeping,
"Noble king, where is my daughter, the blond, the elegant,
The gentle, the courteous, the very cultured one,
Bertha, the noble, who was tenderly reared?
If I do not have news of her soon, I shall go insane! 2170
King, it is not my daughter who was in bed here.
It was Margiste's daughter; may God curse her.
Have her pursued; she may have run away already.
And be sure not to let her mother escape."
Saying this, she fell in a faint in the vaulted room. 2175
And the king, who was crying with pity, got her back up.
From what he heard, he understood the deception.
He saw well how Bertha was exchanged
And saw very clearly that she was betrayed.
Blanchefleur's attendants carried her away, unconscious. 2180
And Pépin was so sad he nearly lost his mind.
"Ah, Bertha," said he, "beautiful sister, sweet friend,
How badly have I behaved toward you!
But they who have betrayed you by their falsity
Will pay for it, by God the Son of Mary. 2185
I know very well that Tybert has murdered you.
He strangled you or cut off your head.
He has conspired with Margiste—may God curse her.
You have been led astray and deceived.
But before the hour of compline comes tomorrow evening 2190
They will know if they have acted foolishly."

XC

The king turned red with anger.
His heart was so sad that he nearly went insane.
He felt pity for Bertha; you should know that if he had known
That she was anywhere in this world, he would have sought for her.   2195
He himself chose four of his men at arms.
He had them take the old woman; each one put a hand on her.
Either by the arm or the dress, each one seized her.
The angriest one smiled.
"Old woman," said the king, "whoever taught and   2200
Instructed you in this treason undertook to shame you.
You should know that he wronged you most evilly;
For you shall be burned, by Jesus Christ."
When the old woman heard it, she trembled with fear.
After this speech, the king left the room.   2205
He went into the hall and sat down on a seat.
He had the noblemen called, and each one came.
When they had come, King Pépin told them
That it would be a good idea to burn the old woman.
"My lord," said his men, "it would be well that she report   2210
What became of Bertha or what she did with her,
If she drowned her or if she murdered her."
And the king replied that it would be good to do it.
The old woman was sent for; no one can contradict it.
When the king saw her, he himself cursed   2215
The one who first had chosen her as a nurse for Bertha.

XCI

When the old woman was taken, she was quite sorrowful and sad.
That day the weather was very ugly with thunder and lightning.
The king was in his golden hall with a painted border.
He asked for the old woman, whose name was Margiste,   2220
And for her daughter, whose name was Bertha in France; but she
Was named Aliste when she was baptized, and she was born at Valgiste.
"Ha, old woman," said the king, "tell, why did you betray
Bertha your gentle lady? Why did you do it?
You know very well that you arranged for your daughter to lie with me.   2225
This was a great falsity. Why did you not confess it?
Even if your body is lost, will you not save your soul?
I certainly believe you undertook the betrayal from your heart.
You are like the people of the Antichrist."

XCII

When the king had had Margiste and Tybert 2230
And the false queen taken, at once their
Evil betrayal was revealed openly.
"Ah, God," said everyone, "why have you tolerated
Such an ugly and cruel murder so long?
How could they have covered it up like this? 2235
Good king, have them punished as they deserve.
If you have pity on them, cursed be the people who serve you."
"Indeed, in faith," said the king, whose heart was sincere,
"Tybert will wipe the main thoroughfare with his back."

XCIII

Tybert and the two servants saw the situation clearly 2240
And that their falsity was completely discovered.
They saw well that for their deeds they would have their just deserts.
"Old woman," everyone said, "how cruel you were
To have made your daughter into Queen Bertha.
You have not succeeded in hiding your deed. 2245
You have murdered our lady; you have brought us great loss,
But you will soon get what you deserve.
How has God tolerated such people for so long?
Blanchefleur, who has a generous heart,
Lifted them from serfdom and complete poverty. 2250
They have not merited it at all; that's for sure."

XCIV

The king saw the two servants and Tybert as well.
You should know that he hated them with his whole heart.
He had the old woman taken first of all.
They pushed her two thumbs into an auger hole at once; 2255
Then they crushed them most painfully.
To make her talk they tortured her greatly.
"Ha, King Pépin," she said, "by God omnipotent,
Let my hands go; I will tell all gladly."
Then they removed the clamp; they did not delay. 2260
And the old woman confessed in the hearing of all the people.
She admitted just how
She had arranged the betrayal from the beginning
And acknowledged as well how she had wanted

To poison Blanchefleur and Pépin 2265
And had provided all the poison.
She was condemned to be burned, and justly.
Afterward Tybert talked quickly and speedily.
"My lord king," said Tybert, "by Saint Vincent,
I did not kill Bertha; you should know that truly. 2270
But I would have killed her—I will not lie about it at all—
If Moran had not forbidden me to do it."
Then he recounted the whole thing,
How Moran had Bertha escape
"Into the woods with the beasts, of which there were many, 2275
Bears, boars and lions, as I have heard.
We left her there in the woods alone.
I believe that she is dead, to the best of my knowledge."
And afterward he told them how
They had given a pig's heart 2280
To Margiste and the false servant—may God destroy her!
He told how tightly and uncomfortably
Bertha was tied with the rope
So that she could not tell how she was suffering
And how he struck her fast and furiously. 2285
All this confirmed the king's suspicions.
More than one thousand seven hundred cried out of pity
When the servant came forward; may God give her grief.
"My lord," she said to the king, "you see well how
All this was not my doing. 2290
It first came from my evil mother,
And because of her we have come to this torment.
May the Lord God who lives in the heavens destroy her."

XCV

All the people who were there were very sad
For the love of their lady, Bertha, the beautiful noblewoman. 2295
They made a great fire of thorny brush; they did not wait long there.
Some stirred up the fire and others fanned it.
The old woman would have all she deserved.
She had entirely merited such payment.
It is right that the one who pursues treachery shall repent. 2300
The old woman was not slow to act treacherously.
Many a winsome young person wept that day
For the love of Bertha; I'm not lying to you.
They threw the stinking old woman into the fire.

Thus was the old woman burned and sent to her death. 2305
When her daughter saw it, she was overcome with fright.
She fell on her face out of fear.

XCVI

When the old woman had been burnt, they hitched up Tybert.
They had him dragged all the way down the main thoroughfare.
At Montfaucon they hanged him high in the wind. 2310
The liegemen and the peers drew aside.
"My lord," they said to the king, "we want to show you
That it is a great thing to be king.
If you want to deal with the servant according to our advice,
Do not have her executed 2315
But allow her to live out her natural life.
Since you have children by her, you must
Have the children and her under your control.
But we feel it is right to say—we do not want to hide it from you—
That from now on she must not ever speak to you or to anyone else 2320
Nor have anything more in the world to do with you."
When the king heard this, he began to sigh.
"My lords," said the king, "by Saint Omer,
She deserves to be destroyed and stoned,
But I hardly want to go against your judgment." 2325
When the servant heard this, she began to praise God.
She had herself taken before the king at once.
When she saw the king, she went to speak to him.
"My lord, please grant me a favor, for the love of God,
That you have me lodged at Montmartre, please. 2330
I would like to become a nun there; I know how to read and sing.
For love of the children you have had by me,
I deserve, my lord, a little special attention.
Give me some of my belongings.
When my sons are grown, I will see that they are married, 2335
And please, my lord, have them knighted
Because they are your children, of that there is no doubt."
And the king granted it; he did not deign to refuse.
Thus went the affair that you have heard me narrate.
The servant had her possessions taken to Montmartre 2340
Loaded onto carts and smaller carts and onto pack horses.
It took eight entire days to assemble her possessions.
There was so much treasure, both silver and bright gold,

Not to mention the other riches I won't even describe.
There were so many that it would be hard to estimate the amount. 2345

XCVII

King Pépin was of very noble character.
Not a king or an emperor had a nobler heart.
The loss of Bertha was sore and bitter to him.
He comforted Blanchefleur, who was overwrought by this calamity,
Who was a mother with a very sad heart for Bertha. 2350
"Ah, daughter," she said, "what will your father say
Who sent you here beautiful and pleasing and radiant?
You were never mean nor stingy toward poor people.
Now Flore has lost both your sister and your brother.
Now may it please God, who is Lord and ruler of 2355
All things, to keep their souls.
I will go toward my lord before daylight tomorrow."

XCVIII

Right beside Blanchefleur, the queen with the fair face,
Sat King Pépin, very sad and pensive.
The people of his country were very sorrowful 2360
That the servant had not been burned or buried.
Blanchefleur did not want to stay in the country any longer.
Her people got her ready; they did not delay.
King Pépin, who was courteous and well brought up,
Did all she wished; he must not be reproached about it. 2365
The next morning at daybreak
They put Blanchefleur the queen on a litter
Between two valuable palfreys,
For her heart was so distressed that she could not ride.
Each one cursed the servant and cried aloud 2370
That Jesus the king of paradise might destroy her
When because of her the noble King Pépin was betrayed
And all the kingdom destroyed and dishonored.
May God curse and destroy her
And her children also, both Rainfrois and Heudris! 2375
Blanchefleur the queen left by way of Saint Denis.
The king accompanied her as far as Senlis.
The next day he departed, sad and distraught.

XCIX

Blanchefleur was going away, grief-stricken.
"Ha, Mother of God," said she, "what sorry shape I am in now! 2380
Bertha, my beautiful daughter, full of nobility,
How sweet and full of goodness you were!
When your father, who truly loves you with all his heart,
Learns the dreadful news from me,
I really believe he will pull out his gray beard. 2385
When he knows how the treachery was undertaken,
There will not be a sadder man from the Holy Land to Friesland.
Alas! Why does my heart not burst under my garments?
Never will I feel joyous, by Saint Denis.
Even if I last until Judgment Day, 2390
I am so sad that I would rather die than live."

C

Then the Hungarians departed; they did not want to wait any longer.
They crossed many lands and many great woods thick with leaves.
Blanchefleur with a very sore heart grieved greatly.
They traveled so many days 2395
That on the Feast of Saint John, a high holy day,
They returned straightaway to Hungary, their country.
They found King Flore, who was greatly distressed
When he had heard the news of his daughter.
He and Blanchefleur greeted one another and wept. 2400
They were so desperate that they could not say a word.
Embracing one another they fell to the ground.
Their people ran to them and raised them back up.
"Ah, God," said King Flore, "what has become of us
When we have thus lost our child Bertha!" 2405
Young and old grieved for Bertha.
"Sweet God," said King Flore, "true Father of King Jesus,
Since it pleases you, dear Lord, to have this befall me,
May you be praised for it, by your sweet spiritual strength,
For when it pleases you, good will be returned to me." 2410

CI

When Blanchefleur came back to her country
And the people of the kingdom had heard the news,
How Bertha of the Big Foot had been deceived,

Many pulled their hair; many beat their palms.
King Flore grieved so that he nearly killed himself, 2415
And Blanchefleur also, who was covered with perspiration.
The people cried hard in every street.
"God," they cried, "what a terrible misfortune
When we have lost the beautiful Bertha this way!
In this land, before she left it, she 2420
Often gave the poor people shoes and new clothing
And fed them many times with her money.
May God who moves the clouds curse
The servant, and Tybert and Margiste, too; for they have certainly crushed
The joy in this land, where it used to flourish! 2425
Now may God absolve Bertha's soul,
For better than she was never seen."

CII

The people of Hungary were very much saddened
For the love of Bertha, who was so kind.
She always was so full of a gracious disposition 2430
That in her kingdom she was always called Her Grace.
I could not tell you, even if I had sworn to do so,
How much the people of Hungary mourned her and regretted her demise
Nor how much they showed their grief.
Blanchefleur told the king and recounted everything, 2435
How Margiste had arranged the treachery.
Weeping, she told him all and described
What happened to Bertha; she did not omit anything,
How she was exchanged in the well-appointed bed
And how Tybert took her away by falsity 2440
And how they had gagged her so that she could not speak,
How Tybert would have cut off her head in the woods
Had it not been for Moran; may God send him joy and health.
He and his companion through nobility
Let Bertha flee into the leafy woods. 2445
There the wild animals killed and devoured her.
Weeping, the king heard every single word.
From deep within his heart he sighed with grief and pity.
Here we shall leave King Flore, whose heart was angry,
And Blanchefleur his wife, whose heart was heavy. 2450
They had often sighed for their daughter Bertha.
Let us speak of King Pépin, the valiant and wise.
When he and Blanchefleur parted

And, weeping, commended one another to Jesus,
He went back to Paris, the admirable city. 2455
Then immediately he ordered Moran and
His two companions to come before him.
And they came willingly and gladly.
They wept with pity for their lady Bertha.

CIII

"Moran," the king said, "now listen to me! 2460
You went with my wife when she was led away.
I know very well that if it had not been for you her head would have been cut off.
I really believe that the wild animals killed and devoured her;
For if she were not dead, she would have returned.
I want you to prepare to go toward Le Mans 2465
And inquire very thoroughly all over the countryside
To find out if any trace of her has been found
Or if anyone saw or met her
After you had left her in the leafy forest.
If I had anything of hers, by the honored Virgin, 2470
Of her or of the clothes that she wore,
You should know that I would love it more than anything in the world,
And I would kiss it morning and evening.
For God who made the sky and the dew, think about it now,
And you will be very well rewarded for your efforts." 2475
"My lord, we will do it since that is what you want."
The next morning they left at daybreak.
They traveled so much along their way, without long pauses,
That they came right to the spot, beside a big valley,
Where Bertha was separated from them for the last time. 2480
Then they cried many tears at that place.
They left there; they did not stay long.
They asked about Bertha all over the countryside.
Throughout the region the word was spread
That the queen of celebrated France was being sought for 2485
And that she had been left, abandoned, in the woods of Le Mans.
They sought for her for fifteen days, but they found nothing of her.
Never did they find of her anything at all.
The news came to Symon the forester,

And Symon told it to his wife Constance. 2490
When Constance heard it, she was concerned.

CIV

"Symon," Constance said, "by the faith that I owe you,
Right in this spot that I hear you speaking of
You found Bertha, I believe.
Let's go talk to her, my lord, together." 2495
"Constance," said Symon, "by all means, I consent."
They called Bertha into a secluded part of the house.
They went to a spot apart from the others; it was just the three of them.
Then Symon, who was full of sincerity, recounted
The calamity and torment, the evil and the disorder 2500
That had befallen the good King Pépin.
"Bertha, as surely as you are standing before me,
Came to the place where I found you.
If you are she, say so, we pray and implore you."
When Bertha heard this, she was greatly frightened. 2505
"My lord," said Bertha, "I have heard and listened to you well,
But I am not she at all; you should know that I am not."

CV

When Bertha heard Symon, she was greatly frightened.
Her whole heart was softened with the news she had heard.
"God," she said in her heart, "keep me on the right path, 2510
My Lord, that I not break my vow.
"Symon," she said, "my lord, why would I hide it from you
If I were queen? I would be committing great folly.
Would to God that I were; it would give me great joy.
You may be sure that I would prefer it 2515
To living here in this wood; I would be insane
If I were queen and then hid it from you.
It would not make any sense to keep myself from being queen.
Rather I would be quite mad if I were lying to you about this."
She did so well at leading them astray 2520
That both acquiesced in what she wanted them to believe.

CVI

Here let us leave the noble, lovely Bertha,
And Symon the forester, who had a valiant heart,

And Constance his wife; may God grant them joy.
Bertha explained all the facts they presented to her 2525
In such a way that they believed what she said.
We will now speak to you about those who were looking for Bertha.
They went throughout the countryside searching for her.
They asked everywhere about what they sought,
But never did they learn a thing. 2530
They returned to Paris, the well-located city.
There they found the king with a sad and sorrowful heart.
And when the king saw them, he called Moran.
And Moran came to him, weeping profusely.
"My lord," said Moran, "by Saint Amant, 2535
We have sought for Madame with all our heart.
All around the forest there is not a living man left,
Knight or bourgeois, serf or peasant,
Woodcutter or coal miner or manual laborer
Not even those who watch over the beasts of the forest 2540
Or church-goer or chapel-goer or traveler passing through the forest
To whom we have not recounted our entire mission.
But now we know less than we knew before."
When the king heard it, what he felt in his heart prompted him to sigh.
And the men at arms left him with sorrowful hearts. 2545

CVII

When King Pépin saw that they would not have news
About his wife Bertha, he revealed his great grief.
Moran was so sorry for having left
His lady in the forest when Tybert led her away,
And his two companions also, that each one of them went on crusade. 2550
To do penance, each one went beyond the seas.
Of these three companions, none returned from overseas
Except just Moran; he came back,
And the others died. You should know that that is how it happened.
Now may God, who created the whole world, have their souls! 2555
One day King Pépin prepared to travel,
To go to Angers, where he had not been for a long time.
He stayed a long time in the region of Anjou.
Right in the time the king was there
Duke Namles came to him—he found him in that place— 2560
To become a knight, which he greatly desired.
He brought with him fully a dozen companions.
Namles knelt before King Pépin

And all the others greeted him.
Duke Namles of Bavaria spoke first: 2565
"Good king," said Namles, "we come to you.
We were born in Germany, in the land beyond here.
I am the son of the Duke of Bavaria; indeed, I will not lie to you.
He sent us to you to become knights.
When we left him, he commanded us very clearly 2570
Not to become knights except by you; that will take place,
Noble, illustrious king, as soon as it pleases you;
And each of us will strive earnestly to serve you."
When the king heard Namles, his esteem for him was strong.
He kept all of them in his service; it pleased him greatly to do so. 2575
He said that he would make them knights at Pentecost;
He would knight them right at the city of Le Mans.
Each one of the young men bowed to King Pépin.
And so Duke Namles lived at the court
With King Pépin and proved himself so well 2580
That he was master of France, and everyone loved him.
Afterward, he gave much good counsel to King Charlemagne.
King Pépin went right to the city of Le Mans.
On the day of Pentecost, he dubbed Namles knight along with all his companions
So that not a single one of them was left out. 2585
And there were as many as one hundred from his own land.

CVIII

The day of Pentecost, as you have heard,
Namles was knighted and many others with him.
Duke Namles had an extremely loyal and bold heart.
Many Turks were later attacked through his boldness 2590
And dead and undone by his good sense.
The king greatly honored them and feted them.
They arranged to have the quintain in a beautiful flowery meadow.
Duke Namles and the others all took part in hitting the target;
Not a one of the newly dubbed knights abstained from it. 2595
The king was in a meadow beneath a leafy pine.
His closest friends came before him:
"My lord," they said to him, "by Saint Remi,
Why will you not take a wife? Will you remain a bachelor all your life?"
"My lords," said the king, "do you know what I say to you? 2600
I loved and cherished my first wife.
It did not please God that I have an heir by her.
Then I took another, from which deed I have had much grief,

Bertha the noble, of whom I saw precious little,
For which reason I have been so grieved 2605
That I will never marry again, of that I assure you.
Now let no one speak to me about it; for I tell you truly,
When I remember Bertha, it nearly kills me.
But since it pleases God who never lies
And his sweet Mother, I thank them from my heart 2610
For all that they send me, and I thank them greatly."
When the noblemen heard him, they were greatly astonished
At words such as these from Pépin.
None spoke afterward; all of them were disconcerted.
When it was time for supper, they did not wait long; 2615
They went back to the city of Le Mans.
The king stayed there until Wednesday.
That very Thursday he went into the forest to hunt.
His party found a big stag; they pursued it.
When the king saw it, he was immensely pleased. 2620
On a good courser he pursued the stag so far
That he lost every one of his companions.

CIX

King Pépin was in the ancient forest.
He was going off through the woods all alone, without company.
I shall leave Pépin a little at this point 2625
And speak of Bertha—may Jesus bless her.
She had lived a long time in this woods
At the home of Symon and Constance, his beloved,
Who had most kindly cared for her along with their daughters.
Beside Symon's house near a meadow 2630
Was a very old chapel
That hermits had built in time gone by.
The chapel came into the hands of an abbey.
There Symon and all his household heard mass.
Its distance from the house was about half a mile. 2635
In the chapel was Bertha, who was very well brought up.
She had hidden herself behind the altar
Where she was offering much heartfelt prayer to God and holy Mary
So that Jesus might give her father and her mother a good life.
She prayed for King Pépin—she did not forget him at all— 2640
That the Lord God guard him from evil and harm;
For the news had been well circulated
That because of her the king often had a sad face

And the people of France were much troubled.
Constance and her two daughters left her there   2645
Because they did not see her at all;
They believed that she had already returned to the house.
There she remained all alone; may God help her,
For shortly she would be extremely upset.

CX

Within the chapel was the beautiful Bertha.   2650
When she realized that she was all alone,
She took her psalter and her book of hours immediately.
She bowed before the altar; then she went outside at once.
And there was King Pépin, who was not going a bit slowly,
Galloping through the forest and searching for his people.   2655
When he saw the maiden, he came right toward her;
And when Bertha saw him, great fear seized her.
The king greeted her with great courtesy;
And Bertha, as a well-mannered person, returned his greeting.
"My beauty," said Pépin, "do not be afraid!   2660
I am one of the people of the king of sweet France.
I have lost my way, and I am dismayed.
Do you know of a house or domain nearby
Where I could get directions?"
"My lord," Bertha said, "by God omnipotent,   2665
Here before us dwells Symon, a worthy man indeed.
He will certainly put you back on the right road, I know."
"My beauty," said Pépin, "I thank you greatly."
When Pépin saw her rosy, blushing face,
For she was white and rose and young and fresh,   2670
His whole heart was aflame with love and desire.
He got off his horse right away;
And Bertha, who expected no harm from it, remained quiet.
The king conversed with her like a gentleman,
And Bertha answered him very thoughtfully.   2675
Immediately the king took her in his arms.
At this, Bertha was greatly chagrined.
She called upon the Lord God, who dwells in the heavens.

CXI

The day was beautiful and clear; it was neither rainy nor windy.
And Bertha was in the woods, distressed, beside Pépin,   2680

She who was very pleasant and young and fresh.
And Pépin was asking her in the name of God to give him her consent
And do his will quickly.
"You will come with me to France, the noble and beautiful land.
You will never see a jewel, no matter how costly it is, 2685
That I will not buy for you if it pleases you.
And if I set you up in the country with a handsome income,
There will not be a man in the land who will torment you about anything."
All of this was not worth so much as a mint leaf to Bertha.
In her heart she blamed herself greatly and lamented so much 2690
Because, alone, she had thus forgotten herself; she regretted it indeed.
King Pépin saw well that she was terrified.

CXII

Bertha, the queen with the fair face, was sorely afflicted.
"Noble man," she said to the king, "for God's sake, leave me alone!
You have made me stay here too long, 2695
For my Uncle Symon must dine very soon
Because after eating he must go to Le Mans
To carry food to the people of the king of France."
"My beauty," said Pépin, "I want to ask you
Who makes you stay here so alone in this wood?" 2700
"My lord," said Bertha, "I do not seek to hide it from you.
See this little chapel here?
I came here today to hear the mass
With my Uncle Symon, whom you heard me mention.
I went all alone into a little corner on the side 2705
To finish reciting my hours; that made him forget me."
When King Pépin heard her speak so sweetly
And saw her so very beautiful that one could see his reflection in her face
—Her face was blushing, beautiful, laughing and bright—
He then began in his heart to desire her ardently. 2710
He remembered the servant; may God give her evil.
It seemed to him that he had never before seen a woman who so resembled the
    other one.
Bertha seemed more beautiful yet to look upon.
Then he could scarcely contain himself, despite whoever might kill him,
So that he could not refrain from making an amorous conquest. 2715
"My beauty," said Pépin, "by Saint Omer,
Do as I wish! I promise you
That I will give you as much wealth as you dare to think of.
I will take you to France to honor you.

I am master of the king who has France to protect. 2720
I am in his good graces more than anyone else; I'm not telling a lie.
You should know that I have so much wealth that I can give you a great deal.
The thing is already done; you never even have to think about it.
You will do my will, whatever it costs."
When Bertha heard this, she began to sigh. 2725
Her beautiful eyes began to weep.
She could see that there was no escape for her
Except to say who she was; she could no longer hold out.
"My lord," she said to the king, "I want to command you
In the name of the Lord who let himself suffer 2730
Upon the holy cross to save his people
Not to lay a hand on Pépin's wife.
I am the daughter of King Flore, of that you must not doubt,
And the daughter of Blanchefleur; may God honor her."
When the king heard it, his color began to change. 2735
From joy in what he heard, he could not say a word.

CXIII

"My lord," Bertha said, "may God and his Mother
Forbid that toward me you have the cruel thought
Of taking my virginity from me.
I am the queen of France; no one must ever doubt it. 2740
I am the wife of King Pépin; King Flore is my father.
Furthermore, Blanchefleur the queen is my mother,
Who is full of all goodness, is not greedy or ungenerous,
But kind and gracious and of noble qualities.
The lady of Saxony is my sister; I also have a brother 2745
Who is the duke of Poland and of the ports of Grodno.
I forbid you in the name of God, who is the true ruler,
To do anything to me which would seem shameful to me.
I would rather be dead, and may God save me."

CXIV

When the king heard what Bertha told him truthfully, 2750
That she was the queen of France, he listened to her very closely;
But in his heart he was extremely worried.
"My beauty," he said, "if it is as you have told me,
I would not do you any harm for a thousand marks of gold."
When Bertha heard this, she took it with much gladness. 2755
In her heart she praised the Lord God greatly.

She turned her face again toward Symon's house.
While going toward it, the king asked
Her many things about her business; but she kept much from him.
She was not concerned about what she told him 2760
Provided that she did not place herself in peril.
In her heart she resolved truly
That never would she go so alone for the rest of her days.
She led King Pépin along talking to him for such a distance
That they entered Symon's house together. 2765
At the entrance they met Symon and Constance,
Isabelle and Aiglente, who had wept
For love of Bertha, who had been gone so long.
They were going to look for her when they saw
That a man was bringing her back, so they stopped. 2770
They saw Bertha's face all frightened;
They saw well that he had not had his way with her.
Now you should know that truly this weighed upon their hearts.
And the king greeted Symon and Constance;
He did not forget Isabelle and Aiglente, 2775
For his heart was very wise and prudent.
They could see quite well that he was a man of great nobility.
He told them that he was with the king of the city of Paris
And that he had lost his way in this leafy wood.
When they heard this, they honored him. 2780
Pépin took Symon; he led him apart a little,
For he wanted to know about the purity of Bertha
As one who had desired her with his whole heart for a long time.

CXV

At Symon's house in the leafy forest
Was the good King Pépin with the valiant air. 2785
When Pépin had told Symon a little of what he was thinking,
Constance was very soon called to this council.
"My lady," the king said, "tell me, if you please,
Who is this maiden that I have brought back here?"
"My lord, she is our niece, whom we have kept a long time. 2790
She has won our love with her goodness.
I love her more than I do my children; may my soul be saved.
She has complained bitterly of you; I am very angry:
You tried to take her virginity by force.
But by the faith I owe to Symon with the graying beard, 2795
If you did not belong to the king of honorable France,

You would have paid for the fright you have given her.
I would rather be dead, if not damned,
Than to have had her virginity stolen from her by you;
For there never lived a wiser woman than she 2800
Nor one who was more completely devoted to God."
When King Pépin heard this, he looked at Constance.
"My lady," said the king, "may the fact not be hidden.
You should know that she has told me such a thing
That, if it is the truth, you will indeed be happy 2805
That you have given her a home for so long.
She let me know that she is called Bertha
And that she is the wife of the king of France the celebrated.
Tell me if it is true without long delay
And be careful that you are not found in a lie, 2810
For you could be shamed and dishonored for it."
When Symon and Constance heard this thing,
They both changed color.
They were very sad that they called her their niece.
"My lord," said Symon, "now listen to me. 2815
Since thus the thing has come and gone
And that she herself has told you,
May God be thanked for it and his Mother praised,
For we knew nothing about it, by the honored Virgin."
Then he told him the time and the day, 2820
How he had found her right at daybreak.
He told him all the trouble, how she was lost
And miserable and suffering with cold and hunger;
And the fictitious information she had given was not forgotten.
He told how she said she had been born and brought up in Alsace 2825
And that she was separated from her country by war
And how she was that night nearly frozen.
"My lord, I tell you the truth that on that morning
She would have died—I really believe it—if she had not been warmed up.
Since then we have fed her and kept her 2830
And we have always called her our niece
Because we did not want people to be suspicious
So that no one would cause her grief.
You should know that she is so wise and well-instructed in all good qualities
And in all her conduct she has so acted 2835
That there is not another woman so worthy in all the country."
When Pépin heard this, he was very much pleased and gladdened.

CXVI

"My lord," said Symon, "by the faith that I owe you,
Since you are one of our king's people,
I am very glad to have you here in my home; 2840
And I have very gladly heard what you have told me.
Never in my life have I had such great joy;
But we knew nothing about it, by Saint Eloi.
We did not believe that it was she.
God help me, I do not know why 2845
She would have hidden it. I am troubled
Because she is wise, without evil and without wrongdoing."
"Symon," said the king, "do you know what I would ask of you?
That we should go speak to her, if you please, the three of us."
"My lord, since it pleases you," said Symon, "I grant it." 2850

CXVII

"My lord," said Symon, "do you know what I would do?
If you would agree, I would go speak to her
And would take Constance my wife with me.
I would hide you very well behind this curtain.
Then I would bring Bertha here to this place at once 2855
And inquire about this thing here, in your hearing.
That is the best thing I can think of, so I advise it."
And the king said it seemed to him a good way to proceed.
So they arranged it since the king granted it.
Symon came to Bertha and took her by the hand, 2860
And Constance gently took her into her bedroom.
"My lady," said Bertha, "I would ask you
What has become of the one, if I dare ask it,
Who gave me so much trouble a while ago when I was coming back
From our chapel? I am still annoyed." 2865
"My beauty, he went away; I won't lie to you.
He told us something that gives us great joy.
Why have you hidden it? My heart is sad."
Bertha looked down at the ground, a little bit ashamed.
Symon sat down next to her; he was very quiet and silent. 2870

CXVIII

"Bertha," said Symon, "by Saint Remi,
That man who just left here

Told us such news, for which the Lord God be thanked,
That we now know that you are the wife of Pépin, the good and powerful king.
You have hidden it a long time; certainly that worries me. 2875
You would have been more honored and served if we had known."
"My beauty," said Constance, "there is no reason to lie;
But tell the truth; for God's sake, I pray you."
When Bertha heard this, she blushed.
She responded very courteously at once. 2880
"My lady, previously," she said, "you have said this to me.
From that time on, if I had been she, I would have said so.
Indeed, I would have the first day that I ever came here.
You see, it is the only way I could find mercy
From the man who assailed me today in the woods. 2885
If I had not done it, I believe I would have been dishonored;
But by this lie I saved myself from him.
I told him that I was the wife of Pépin, the bold king,
And the daughter of King Flore, a very lordly king.
Indeed, I had heard how people betrayed 2890
The gracious and courteous queen of France
And how she was left in the leafy woods.
As soon as I told him that, he immediately left me alone.
I did not see any other evasion that would protect me.
I thought of this trick; the Lord God be thanked for it." 2895

CXIX

Bertha was in the room, the noble, the elegant.
With her were Symon and his beloved Constance.
King Pépin was there, but she did not know it at all.
They talked to Bertha about many things
And often questioned and strongly confronted her with them. 2900
She feared angering God and holy Mary.
Therefore, she didn't want them to know anything at all about it.
Constance took her back to another part of the house.
She left her in a room with her daughters.
Then she went right back to Symon. 2905
There she found the king, whose grief was written on his face.
"My lord," said Constance, who was perceptive,
"I do not know what you have to say about this; but I am completely puzzled.
My goodness, if it were she, I would be simply astounded.
If she were hiding it, that would be insane. 2910
From what I have heard, I do not know what to say to you."

Then the king got up, but he had no desire to laugh.
He took his leave of Constance; he did not want to delay any longer.
And Symon — may Jesus bless him — escorted him.
He took him straight back to Le Mans, and the king abandoned the hunt. 2915
At that hour, hunting was of very little concern to him.

CXX

When King Pépin was a good distance from the house,
He spoke to Symon, who was very wise.
"Symon," he said to him, "you do not know me.
I am King Pépin, you should truly know." 2920
When Symon heard it, he was joyous and glad.
As was fitting, Symon bowed to him.
"My lord," Symon said, "you are very welcome!
I am sad at heart that I was so deceived
That I did not recognize you. I am very sorry 2925
That you were not appropriately honored in my house."
"Don't worry," said the king, "I count myself well served
Except that I am upset about the queen, my wife,
Who by great mischance and misfortune has been taken from me."
Then the king spoke often to Symon. 2930
All their talk was about Bertha of the Big Foot.

CXXI

"Symon," said the king, "do you know what you will do?
When I come near Le Mans, you will go back.
Be careful not to speak to anyone about this
Except for your wife. You will keep very quiet about it. 2935
For you should know that in my heart I am persuaded
That this is my wife; you are mistaken to doubt it
Because she denies it. I am very worried."
"My lord," said Symon, "you should never believe me again
If I am wrong now: she is your wife Bertha that you love so much. 2940
When I found her in the woods, she was very poor.
She was starving; she was frozen.
Perhaps she made some vow at that point
About why she must hide her situation.
And, if she took this vow, make no mistake, 2945
She would not break it for all the gold of ten cities;
For a more honorable woman than she never lived."

"Symon," said the king, "you are indeed astute.
I believe quite truly that you have spoken the truth.
But you should know that I have been deceived by a woman   2950
And because of that this must be of the greatest certainty.
I will send word to King Flore, who is valiant and wise,
And Blanchefleur, too—neither of them will be forgotten—
How I met Bertha in this woods.
I know well that one of them will soon be coming here.   2955
Either tonight or tomorrow a messenger will be prepared
To carry a message to Hungary.
As soon as I can, you will see me again.
Be sure that not a word about this thing is said.
Give your wife Constance my cordial greetings.   2960
And as for Bertha, I implore you that you honor her more
Than you did before if you love me at all."
"My lord, that is what I will do since you wish it."
Symon went so far with the king
That the king found many of his people again.   2965
By the king's command, Symon turned back.
The king sweetly commended him to Jesus.
He went back to his home, which was called Florimés.
He recounted what had happened to Constance.
Constance praised the Lord God greatly for this.   2970
She kissed and hugged Symon with joy.
The king went into the city of Le Mans.
When he got off his horse, he did not stop there.
He called a chaplain who was one of his intimates.
He had him write a letter for him, which was sealed immediately.   2975
On that same day the messenger started out.
May the Lord God, the king of majesty, be his guide.

CXXII

The messenger went away; he hastened at all speed,
For the good King Pépin pleaded with him to do so with all his heart.
He told him that upon his return, he would make him a rich man.   2980
The king returned to the city of Paris.
With him went Duke Namles, whom he loved devotedly.
He honored him and his companions greatly.
The messenger upon his journey rode and traveled so much
That he found the king of Hungary in his land.   2985
With him was Blanchefleur, who had an abundance of all good qualities.
The messenger knelt right in front of King Flore.

He greeted him and also the queen at that moment on behalf of King Pépin.
Then he gave them the letter.
The king broke the wax; he turned the letter over. 2990
Before he spoke, he called the queen.
"Blanchefleur, sweet love," said he, "listen to this!
God will be praised for the news we have here.
It is certainly right that many hearts will have great joy over this."
The king read the letter; he left nothing out. 2995
It told exactly what had happened,
How King Pépin was hunting in the woods,
How he met the lovely Bertha in the woods,
And the reason why he had left her there.
He truly believed that it was she, but he left her there 3000
Until King Flore could identify her
Or Blanchefleur, her mother. By heaven, now we'll see
If one or the other ever loved Bertha.
The king and the queen looked at one another.
They were so overwhelmed with joy that neither of them spoke. 3005
From joy and pity King Flore wept.
The queen trembled all over with joy.
The king lifted up Blanchefleur in his arms.
When she was able to speak, she did not stop.
She said that she would never stay in a city for more than one night 3010
Until she could kiss Bertha's mouth.
Blanchefleur knew so well that it was Bertha that she would never have doubts.
Her heart told her that it was the truth; she would be well assured of it.
"My lady," said the king, "never fear.
If my name is King Flore, I will go with you 3015
And whoever else will go, tomorrow at the crack of dawn, if it please God."
When the lady heard it, she thanked him profusely.
King Flore prepared for the journey right away
In order to travel the next day; thus he commanded it.
The queen got up; she embraced the messenger. 3020
In the view of those who were there she sweetly kissed him.
The next day King Flore mounted his horse very early in the morning.
He brought along with him many high nobles.
He traveled so many days and so expeditiously
That he came to Paris. The king and his barons 3025
Showed great joy; each one honored him
And Blanchefleur, for there was good reason to do it.

CXXIII

King Pépin most nobly received
The good king of Hungary, who had white hair,
And Blanchefleur his wife, the best woman that ever was.   3030
They recalled many things to one another then.
"King Pépin," said the lady, "for the love of God, the King Jesus,
Let us hasten to our destination."
"My lady," said Pépin, "we have waited too long;
But tomorrow, if it please God, we will go in the morning early."   3035
They stayed in the city of Paris only one night.
They traveled so far that they came to Le Mans
At the dinner hour; at least that is what I heard.
But Blanchefleur neither ate nor drank;
Her heart was aflutter for love of her daughter.   3040
She would never rest until sure proof had been established.
If it were Bertha, her daughter, she would recognize her right away.
And there appeared Symon, the good forester.
He went toward King Pépin; he greeted him courteously.
And when the king saw him, he recognized him right away.   3045
He led him away into a place apart.

CXXIV

"My lord," said Symon, "has Blanchefleur come?"
"Yes," said the king, "but she is so distraught
That she cannot sleep or drink or eat;
She will have no joy until she has identified Bertha.   3050
You should know that if it is her daughter that you have had,
You can very well say that your honor is increased."
"My lord," said Symon, "may my soul be absolved.
It is Bertha your wife, whom you must love very much,
Good king, that you have seen in my house.   3055
Many times since I have reasoned with her about it.
As soon as I bring it up, her color changes.
She does not want to answer me; she is so silent and mute.
She is so frightened that she trembles all over.
So help me God,   3060
There is not a more noble woman on earth."
When the king heard it, it gave him great joy.
"Symon," said the king, "this will be known soon.

Right now let us make our way
Straight to your house in the leafy forest. 3065
We are going to find great joy; we have pursued it well.
May God grant that we find it; we have long awaited it."

CXXV

King Pépin was a very wise and thoughtful man.
He sent for King Flore and Blanchefleur at once,
And they came, ready to get on their way. 3070
They went out of the city in a private group,
And Symon, who was full of kindness, accompanied them.
Pépin concealed well from Flore and Blanchefleur
That he was the worthy man who had kept their daughter
Until such time as they could know the truth for certain. 3075
In this fashion they went together through the leafy wood.
They did not stop until they reached Symon's house.
This was what Blanchefleur the queen wanted.
They entered the house all together.
Symon came to Constance and asked her, 3080
"My fair companion, where is Bertha, for goodness sake?
Here is King Pépin, whom I have brought to her,
And Flore and Blanchefleur, in whom there is much goodness."
"My lord," said Constance, "may God be pleased by what we are doing today.
She is sitting in my room, actually, 3085
Where she has been working hard since this morning
On our altar cloth, which she found torn."

CXXVI

When Symon the forester had heard his wife,
He called King Flore with the gray beard and
Pépin and Blanchefleur; he did not delay. 3090
He led them into the room, which was unlocked.
There they found the noble Bertha.
When she recognized them, she rose immediately.
As soon as she recognized her mother, she knelt at her feet;
And Blanchefleur fell to the floor in a faint from joy. 3095
"God help me," said Flore, "our honored Lady,
It is my daughter Bertha that I have found here.
God through his great goodness has restored her to us."
King Flore took Bertha, whom he had yearned for so much, in his arms.
Sweetly he kissed her and tightly embraced her. 3100

Blanchefleur got back up; she took Bertha from his arms.
She could not get enough of kissing her.
When the people gathered together there
Once knew how they had recovered joy,
You would have heard them cry out with shouts of gladness. 3105
Such joy as that was never before seen or envisioned.
"Ah, God," said Pépin, "who made the sky and the dew,
My Lord, may you be praised for this good outcome!
I have gladly borne my misfortune for you according to your will,
And you have very well rewarded me for it; 3110
For you have transformed my tribulation into great joy.
For never in my life have I had the least bit of joy
That is not now turned into a hundred doubles doubled.
May the one who bore you in holiness
Be now in this day thanked and praised." 3115
Quickly the news traveled to Le Mans.
All the king's people hastened there as if crazed.
There was not a bell in the city that did not ring.

CXXVII

When Bertha saw her father and her mother, too,
She felt such great joy—I'm telling you the truth— 3120
That she could scarcely say a word; her heart failed her entirely.
Pépin came up to Bertha; he did not wait long.
"Sweet love," said he, "for God's sake, speak to me.
I am King Pépin, who implores your pity
Although I never in my life deserved it." 3125
Bertha was struck with amazement when she heard him.
As one reared quite well she answered fittingly.
"My lord, if it is you, I thank the Lord God who was
Born of the holy Virgin in Bethlehem."
Blanchefleur and King Flore greeted 3130
The noble Bertha with a hundred times more joy and effusion than I am describing.
I have never heard any man speak of any greater joy
Than was had that day at Symon's house in the leafy woods.
King Pépin called one of his men at arms, Henri,
Gautier his marshal, and Thierri his chamberlain: 3135
"Go at once to Le Mans; don't be slow;
Have tents brought because that is what I wish.
I shall remain in this place, by Saint Remi.
I have found joy again here that I have not experienced for a long time.
Now provide for us well, for we shall remain here. 3140

Have Namles come; this I order and implore you."
They, who were so eager to carry out his wishes, went away.
And so they arranged everything. This was on a Monday.

CXXVIII

Blanchefleur was filled with joy again
Since she held her daughter in her arms, 3145
Bertha, the well-reared, the blond, the elegant.
She hugged and kissed her many a time that day.
Before them came Symon and his love Constance,
Isabelle and Aiglente, whom Bertha did not hate a bit.
When Bertha saw them, she leapt up at once. 3150
"Mother," said Bertha, "for the sake of God, the Son of Mary,
Here is the sweet lady who has tenderly cared for me,
And here is my lord, may Jesus bless him,
Who found me alone in the ancient forest.
I know very well, if he had not come to me, I would be dead or devoured. 3155
After God, they saved me from death.
You should know that, if it were not for them, I would not be alive."
When Blanchefleur heard this, she stood up to meet them.
So did King Flore, the lord of Hungary.
They rejoiced most heartily and truly in greeting 3160
Constance and Symon, the forester with the white beard.
And behold King Pépin, whose face was happy.
Together they sat down in the vaulted room.
Now this room was certainly filled with joy.

CXXIX

In the beautiful forest—I don't want to lie to you— 3165
They showed great joy at the home of Symon the forester.
They had many different kinds of tents set up.
They rejoiced greatly; there is no need to elaborate about this.
That night Pépin lay with his wife.
They stayed there three days; that's what I have heard. 3170
A daughter was conceived, no doubt.
Her name was Gisela; she was the mother of Roland, the good warrior.
Afterward he begat Charlemagne, the good and righteous king.
Pépin had Symon equipped,
And he made knights of him and his two sons, each one of them. 3175
He had each of them given coats of fine cloth of gold
Well suited to their wishes, just as they wanted them.

The king made Symon his master counselor.
Duke Namles went to them to put on their spurs
And good King Pépin fastened large steel swords around their waists. 3180
He dubbed each one knight; then he went to kiss them.
When Symon saw so much honor heaped upon himself,
He began in his heart to thank God with all his might.
His two children and he went to kneel
Before King Pépin to thank him, 3185
And they wanted to kiss his foot and his leg.
And the king himself raised them back up on their feet.
"Symon," said the king, "by Saint Richier,
I am bound to love you and Constance and hold you dear,
For you have certainly put my heart at ease with joy. 3190
By the grace of God, the just Father,
You have preserved my wife from mortal pain."
Whoever might have seen Blanchefleur, the lady with the loyal heart,
Kiss Constance and her two daughters and hold them tightly
And weep from pity and joy at the same time 3195
Would certainly have said that this was the joy of one's desire.

CXXX

Constance was very wise and well-mannered;
She was indeed an excellent woman and very good almsgiver.
She saw that Symon and her children had glad faces.
Each one had a coat with good, costly feathers. 3200
She thanked the Lord God and the worthy Saint Peter for it.
"Ha, Lord God," said she, "gentle king, true giver of justice,
You do us more honor than we deserve.
I thank our Lady, the just Lady, for it.
Certainly we who were in wretched brush are put in a beautiful meadow. 3205
For those from whom it comes I will pray many a prayer.
If it please God and I am able, I will not be slow about it."

CXXXI

You have already heard how our good King Pépin
Knighted Symon, that he loved so much,
Along with his two sons, to whom he showed great love. 3210
He gave large gifts to all three, to Symon and his two sons.
He presented Symon with a thousand pounds' worth of landholdings
And five hundred pounds' worth of favorably located land to each of his sons.
He said that he would see that Isabelle and Aiglente were married.

He would give five hundred pounds a year to each one of them. 3215
And Symon, above all, did not forget his duties the least bit.
He and his two sons, all three came forward and knelt down.
Constance and her two daughters did not tarry.
All three knelt, bowing to the king.
Each one thanked the king in the name of the Lord God. 3220
There they became his men; they all kissed him in faithfulness.
The king devised the arms they carried.
The master made them of azure, but with
A few white figures here and there because he was ordered to do it.
There was a large gold fleur-de-lis in the center. 3225
The older son wore it with five labels of gules.
The silver label of the younger son bore bezants.
The king—may Jesus, who created the whole world, protect him—
Had them bear these arms for the sake of the love he bore them.
Since then their lineage has borne and will bear them. 3230
Those who inherited them bear them still.

CXXXII

After Symon was thus knighted
And the king had given him large domains,
All the noblemen left Florimés.
Queen Bertha sighed many sighs 3235
Upon leaving, for she had lived there for a long time.
She was there nine and a half years; it's the truth.
You should know that not a single person remained in the house,
Not a valet or servant, foreign or domestic,
To whom great gifts were not given on behalf of the queen. 3240
Blanchefleur and King Flore did not forget any one at all.
They gave them so much that they would never be poor.
And Symon and Constance both left
As did their sons and daughters; not a one remained.
Upon their departure—believe it— 3245
The household uttered many a pitiful cry.
Many a palm was beaten and many a lock of hair pulled.
"Ah, gentle lady, farewell," they said, "you are going away.
May you be commended to the Lord God of glory.
May he render unto you the wealth that you have given us!" 3250
Weeping, Bertha—may God increase his kindness to her—went away
With Constance and her daughters close beside.
"Constance," said Bertha, "you will come away with me.
In the land of France you will never leave me.

Give me your daughters Isabelle and Aiglente. 3255
Never will I have riches while they are poor."
"My lady," said Constance, "so be it as you have said.
It is certainly right that we do all you wish."

CXXXIII

On a Tuesday morning, you should know it truly,
Many a person left Florimés joyously, 3260
For their lady, the lovely Bertha, was being brought back from it.
Those from Le Mans came to meet them joyfully.
They greeted their lady properly and courteously.
King Flore and Namles also accompanied her.
Beside her was her mother, who gazed at her often. 3265
This day lances made a great fracas.
All the bells of the city rang loudly.
The clergy came to meet them in excellent order
In a big procession beautifully and properly.
There were reliquaries and incense burners of gold and silver. 3270
The countryside was resplendent with cloth of gold and silk.
All the people in the whole country had come.
Ladies and knights came nobly
To become acquainted with their lady, which they greatly desired to do.
They entered at once into the city of Le Mans. 3275
The streets were beautifully and richly covered.
The pavement of the streets was strewn thickly
With fresh grass and reeds everywhere.
The ladies at the windows were elegantly dressed.
That day you could see many a fine garment. 3280
I will not give you a long account of this.
The queen descended at the steps of the palace.
Namles and the noblemen kindly accompanied her.
They took her mother, who loved her ardently, by the hand.
There were great festivities in the city for eight whole days. 3285
The news spread throughout the kingdom
That Bertha had been found; people often thanked
God and his sweet Mother and the saints also.
They departed from Le Mans; they did not stop there.
They went joyously away to the city of Paris. 3290

CXXXIV

Then the two kings were going away, they did not wait any longer,
And Blanchefleur and Bertha, whom it pleased greatly.
Near them were Constance, Isabelle, and Aiglente.
They rode joyously; nothing worried them.
They went straight toward Paris, the noble and lovely city.   3295
The contemptible servant—may God destroy her—
Heard the news; she was extremely sorry.
She was strongly displeased; she very much did not want this to happen.
She was terrified; she was scared out of her wits.
She was heartily sorry that the king had given Symon a living.   3300
She was grieved when good succeeded, the filthy, stinking servant.
God gave her what she deserved for her false behavior!

CXXXV

In all the cities that Bertha went through
The people came from everywhere to meet her
In great processions; each one honored her greatly.   3305
They prayed to God, who sits high and sees far,
That he destroy the servant, wherever she might be,
Both her and the children that she had borne
When because of her Bertha had been lost for so long.
Throughout the kingdom there was so much joy   3310
For the love of their lady that God had sent back
That they ran to her throughout the country
On foot and on horseback so that none stayed away.
They believed that whoever could see her would feel greatly rewarded.
It is not a great marvel that people wanted her   3315
For the good news that everyone told about her
And for the beautiful miracle that God had demonstrated through her.
As the queen approached, everyone knelt
And thanked God for her return.
And she, as was proper, bowed to them.   3320

CXXXVI

The queen of France was very wise and clever.
Each one because of her goodness wished to see her.
Then Blanchefleur was indeed at ease in the straight road.
She thanked our Lady, the blessed Lady.
They traveled in short journeys; they did not make too great haste.   3325

The minstrels created joy, for each one wanted to be with her.
Whoever caused the most joy believed that he was doing the best that could be done.
The old woman was false and mean and traitorous
Who betrayed her lady in secret.
May her daughter, the filthy, tormented servant, be cursed! 3330
The road to paradise would be very narrow,
If she never repented of such accursed work.

CXXXVII

In France the young and the old had great joy.
Pépin's friends and confidants came to meet him
And to meet their lady, who gave them great joy; 3335
And they greatly thanked Jesus that she had been found.
They traveled so far that many a bell of Paris was in view.
Paris was ornamented as never before,
For the people were much moved with great joy
For the goodness that they saw God had rendered unto them. 3340
Neither the bald nor those with hair remained in the city.
Neither was there monk nor abbot, ordained or cloistered,
Who did not all come in procession.
You should know that on this day many great coursers ran
And many a lance was broken on a shield. 3345
The noble Bertha had many greetings on this day.

CXXXVIII

The queen of France came to Paris,
And many a person most gladly saw her there.
Nobly they led her down the main thoroughfare.
"Ah, God," said each one, "holy Mary, help! 3350
May the filthy servant be struck with an evil death
Who caused such a sweet lady to be lost so long!"
Bertha got down at the steps of the hall.
Then Blanchefleur was indeed moved with great joy
When she saw her daughter received like this 3355
And saw how each one had great joy because of her,
She thanked the Lord God, who makes the clouds move across the sky,
Him and his sweet Mother; she did not hold back from thanking God.
They kept up the festivities at Paris for eight days.
There will never be nobler or richer ones. 3360

CXXXIX

King Pépin was an extremely kind and courteous man.
With all his heart he strove to honor King Flore
And also Blanchefleur, who was very praiseworthy.
Right on a Sunday after dinner
Here came Moran, who was returning from beyond the seas. 3365
When he saw the king, he went to greet him.
The news he heard recounted gave him so much joy
That he could scarcely say a word to the king.
"My lord," said Moran, "may God be praised
Because you once again have Madame, the queen with the fair face! 3370
Alas! I would never dare to go before her;
For I was one of those, I cannot conceal it,
Who led her into the woods to shame her."
Then Moran began to cry hard.
"Moran," said the king, "you are not to blame; 3375
For because of you she escaped; I have been assured of that."
A messenger went at once to tell the queen;
When the queen heard it, she did not want to delay any more.
In sight of everyone she went to hug Moran's neck.
"My lord," she said to the king, "I would like to ask a favor of you. 3380
It is that you love Moran with all your heart
And have him knighted now,
And give him so much of your wealth
That his heirs after him can support themselves with it.
If it had not been for him, I would be dead—I can swear it on the 3385
    saints—
When Tybert the traitor wanted to cut off my head.
I will put my trust in Symon and him always
And act upon their counsel in all my affairs."
When the king heard this, he did not want to refuse it.
He settled two hundred marks a year upon him. 3390
And Moran, who was wise and very praiseworthy,
Went to kiss the king's shoe,
And he went to bow on his knees to the queen.
King Pépin had him equipped the next day.
Moran became a knight, as you have heard me tell. 3395
Blanchefleur and King Flore had Moran presented with
Great wealth on behalf of their daughter, whom they had heard speak of him.
For this reason, everyone should remember that it is good to do good deeds.
For in the long run, goodness triumphs.

CXL

"Moran," said the queen, "I was very much afraid that day 3400
When Tybert was holding the sword, which was sharp and bright.
He wanted to cut my head off.
I found you full of pity and of good character.
If you had had any cruel thought towards me
Such as Tybert had, who was a traitor and a thief, 3405
Never would I have seen my sweet, dear mother
Nor the king of France nor King Flore, my father.
You were loyal, and I found you to be a friend like a brother.
I will never be miserly when it comes to rewarding you."
"My lady," said Moran, "may God our true Savior 3410
Reward you, very kind lady."

CXLI

There was great joy in the city of Paris.
King Pépin honored King Flore very much
Along with Blanchefleur; he held them very dear.
After the king had knighted Moran, 3415
King Flore only stayed a month more in the kingdom.
I will not set out and enumerate for you at length
Either the gifts or the riches that were presented
To the Hungarians by King Pépin
And the queen, who was very kind. 3420
On a Thursday morning they prepared to travel.
They sighed many a sigh upon leaving Paris.
King Flore and Blanchefleur commended to God
All the people, each and every one, that had met them.
They blessed them all, foreign and domestic. 3425
King Pépin of France and Bertha of the wise heart
Accompanied them as far as Saint Quentin.
They stayed there only two days.

CXLII

Right at Saint Quentin, it is the proven truth,
Blanchefleur departed from Bertha the wise. 3430
King Flore kissed and hugged his daughter.
They took leave of her; they commended her to God.
And Bertha the queen fainted.
Sweetly the king comforted her.

And the Hungarians went away at once. 3435
They went through many a land, many a foreign country.
They journeyed so far that the came to their land; they brought back joy
For which God and his Mother were praised.
After their return, that very year
They had a daughter; they named her Constance 3440
For the love of Constance, who had protected their daughter,
As you have heard, in the leafy forest.
She was afterward declared queen of Hungary.
The Danes threatened her with war, which disturbed her greatly.
I will not tell you any more about this. 3445
King Flore, who was very wise,
And Blanchefleur also, the lauded queen,
Founded a beautiful abbey in the country
In honor of Jesus, who made the sky and the dew,
For love of Bertha that God had brought back 3450
And who had escaped from such peril.
They also established sixty nuns there.
The abbey is still called Valbertha.
Here I will leave King Flore of the gray beard
And Blanchefleur; may God crown her soul. 3455
And I shall speak of Pépin of cherished renown
And of Bertha—may God give her a good future—
Who remained distressed with grief for her father and mother
After she, weeping, was parted and separated from them.
They came back to Paris; they did not delay a long time. 3460

CXLIII

King Pépin and his gracious, distinguished wife
Came back to Paris. They did not delay long there.
The king greatly loved Symon and Constance his wife
And welcomed them with great honor; they had well deserved it.
The king arranged marriages for Isabelle and Aiglente 3465
So that each one was established with great nobility.
The servant who had betrayed her lady was at Montmartre.
With her were her children, both Rainfrois and Heudris.
The servant reared them in lordly fashion.
Afterward many people were mistreated by the two of them 3470
Because of the great wealth they had,
As you will be able to hear if I tell you the story.

CXLIV

The first of the children—do not doubt it a bit—
That the king had by Bertha, the blond, the elegant,
Was a girl, wise and well brought up.   3475
She was the wife of Milon d'Aiglent; she was of great nobility
And was the mother of Roland, who was without cowardice.
Rather he was valiant and bold, full of chivalry.
Afterward she had Charlemagne of the bold face,
Who later made many a great attack on pagans.   3480
By him the law of God was held up and exalted.
By him pagans were exiled from many a land,
Many a helmet split, many a shield pierced,
Many a hauberk broken, and many a head cut open.
He fought with great courage against the pagan people,   3485
So much so that the people of that race still grieve.

Here ends *Bertha of the Big Foot*.

Notes

Among the notes below are reproduced (as I have translated them) several of Albert Henry's notes from *Berte as grans piés*, the contents of which cannot be indicated in the translation of the narrative itself, and which may aid the reader's understanding. The items in brackets are my explanatory additions.

The saints referenced below often appear to be invoked because their names fit conveniently with the rhyme scheme of their *laisses* (stanzas). The reader may wonder if some of them came to Adenet's mind because of their work in France, particularly in northern France and in the regions north of France where Adenet lived. Others' names might have come up frequently in religious services. A few are called upon for their special efficacy in protecting against specific dangers.

pages 4 and 5: Curses, particularly those invoking divine destruction, appear very sparingly in the following twelfth- and thirteenth-century works: *La Chanson de Roland, Gormont et Isembart, La Chanson de Guillaume, Lais* (Marie de France), *Le Chevalier de la charette, Le Pèlerinage de Charlemagne, Tristan en prose* (first part), *La Quête del Saint Graal, Guiron le Courtois*. Béroul's *Tristan* (1165–1200), 4,485 lines, contains at least thirteen curses, five of which invoke God's destruction. *La Chanson d'Aspremont* (1185–1190) at 11,376 lines is nearly four times as long as *Berte* and contains thirteen curses, nine of which ask for God's destruction. In *Ami et Amile* (1200), 3,504 lines, God is asked on seven occasions to curse, destroy, or to help someone kill another. *Florence de Rome* (early thirteenth century), 4,562 lines, contains nine curses, five requesting God's destruction. *Aye d'Avignon* (about 1200), 4,136 lines, has fifteen curses, nine calling for God's annihilation. *Parise la duchesse* (second quarter of the thirteenth century), 3,157 lines, has twenty-one curses, twelve of which want God to destroy someone.

pages 5 and 6: Leslie Z. Morgan points out that confusion about events in various versions of Bertha's story may partially result from the large number of Bertas who were wives of Merovingian and Carolingian kings. Certainly, Pépin had a wife named Bertrade, who was the mother of Charlemagne; but keeping her attributes straight might present difficulty. A Queen Berta with a foot deformity appears in literature and art in the thirteenth century. In the *Geste Francor*, the

Franco-Italian version of Pépin's wife's story, the treatment of the deformity reveals the folk belief that such abnormalities resulted from the sins of the parents or of the society to which the child belonged and that evil traits persisted in the child. Adenet's version, produced within a different culture of beliefs, makes no suggestion of such ideas.[1]

page 10: In the well-known poem "Ballade des dames du temps jadis" by the fifteenth-century French poet François Villon, Bertha's name is mentioned among the women of former times of whose whereabouts the poet inquires: "Berthe au grand pied, Biétris, Alis . . . ." He answers his question with the refrain, "Mais où sont les neiges d'antan?" ("But where are the snows of yesteryear?")[2]

lines 7–15, 155, 202, 903–904, 1388, 1803, 1823, 2389, 2376: The abbey and church of Saint-Denis (in the suburb of the same name just north of Paris) was the repository of the history of the kings of France, officially begun in the twelfth century by the illustrious advisor to the kings of France and abbot of Saint-Denis, Suger. The histories continued to be written at Saint-Denis in Latin until 1286. In the thirteenth and fourteenth centuries, they were written in French and given the title *Les Grandes Chroniques de France*. Since the seventh-century Merovingian king Dagobert, who bequeathed it his library and had himself buried there, Saint-Denis had become the royal abbey and basilica and the burial place of most French kings, whose sculpted effigies lie atop their tombs. French kings from Dagobert onward, particularly Charlemagne, had given rich gifts to Saint-Denis and attracted scholars to its school and scriptorium. Centuries before Suger made the *Chroniques* official (and rebuilt the structures of the basilica and abbey in Gothic styles that became models for European architecture), the monks of the abbey had written chronicles of the kings of France. By the twelfth century, Saint-Denis was famous as a seat of culture.[3] It was indeed an important information source for serious writers, including apparently for some *trouvères* whose characters were kings (Nebbiai-Dalla Guarda, *Bibliothèque*, 50). However, in his note to line seven of *Berte aus grans piés*, Henry comments on the jongleur's common practice of lending an air of authenticity to his tales by insisting that his information comes from the books at Saint-Denis, telling us meanwhile that his efforts to track down the actual existence of the Saint-Denis monks Adenet

---

[1] Leslie Z. Morgan, "*Berti ai piedi grandi*: Historical Figure and Literary Symbol," *Olifant* 19 (1994–1995), 39–45.

[2] François Villon, *Oeuvres: Traduction en français moderne accompagnée de notes explicatives*, Tome I, *Le Lais–Le Testament. Première partie*, trans. André Lanly (Paris: Librairie Honoré Champion, 1978), 83.

[3] Donatella Nebbiai-Dalla Guarda, *La Bibliothèque de l'abbaye de Saint-Denis en France du IXe au XVIIIe siècle* (Paris: Editions du Centre National de la Recherche Scientifique, 1985), 17–50.

mentions in his works have been futile. Henry refers there to this tendency, with some apparent annoyance, as a "Véritable tic de jongleur . . ." ("The minstrel's downright bad habit . . .").[4] Saint Denis is named for the patron saint of France, a missionary to Paris and its first bishop. Rebel heathen martyred him by beheading about 258 A.D. According to a ninth-century legend, he picked up his severd head and walked two miles with it to Montmartre.[5] His name is invoked in lines 1803, 1823, and 2389, in a feminine form in the latter two instances to accord with the rhyme. In each of these three instances, he is called upon in a moment of great emotional stress (the second time, the stress results from the narrator's anger with the behavior of the evil servants). Lines 155 and 2376 refer to the suburb of Saint-Denis.

lines 26–32: "Allusion to one of the versions of the *chanson de geste Girart de Roussillon*" (*Berte*, 175).

lines 33–35: "The Vandals figure notably in *Girart de Roussillon* and in *Garin le Lorrain*; here, Adenet seems to be remembering the geste of the Lorrains" (*Berte*, 175).

line 38: "The epics designate the palace of the king (in the *Ile de la Cité*) by the words *palais* [palace] or *sale* [hall] (the latter often qualified by *voutie* [vaulted] or by *listée* [ornamented with a border]; compare, for example, below, line 2219)" (*Berte*, 176).

lines 89–100: "Pépin first married Blanchefleur: Gerbert, Gérin and Malvoisin are several of the principal Lorrains, relatives of the queen. Adenet recalls, in lines 92–95, the battle of the Lorrains against Fromont and his Bordelais. Recollections of *Garin le Lorrain* and especially of *Gerbert de Metz*" (*Berte*, 176).

lines 108, 2323, 2716: Saint Omer (Audomar) was born about 600 at Guldenal, Switzerland, into a noble family. After the death of his mother, he and his father entered the abbey of Luxeuil in the diocese of Besançon, where Omer did well in the study of scripture. He was chosen to serve when King Dagobert asked for a bishop for Thérouanne, principal city in the territory of the Morini in Neustria. Saint Omer and helpers sent from Luxeuil were a third wave of missionaries sent to the Morini. Their efforts once again established Christianity among these in-

---

[4] Adenet le Roi, *Berte aus grans piés*, ed. Albert Henry (Paris: Presses Universitaires de France, 1963), 200.

[5] Richard P. McBrien, *The Lives of Saints* (San Francisco: HarperSanFrancisco, 2003), 414.

habitants. Saint Omer built a church and two monasteries. The town of Saint Omer in the north of France is named for him. He died about 670.[6]

line 222: The phrase "a nun's habit" is used to translate the word *saie*, a coarse cloth, which Henry tells us "was often dyed black and was used, notably, to make religious habits" (*Berte*, 176).

lines 258, 2034: Perhaps the Saint Clement here (Climent in the poem) refers to the fourth-century bishop of Rome who wrote a letter in 96 A.D. to the Christians at Corinth, an important document in church history. No facts support the legend that he was enslaved and taken to Crimea where he worked in the mines and was martyred by drowning with an anchor tied around his neck. However, in the Middle Ages, the letter to Corinth was not as well known as the tales of his martyrdom.[7]

line 342: "'The garden of the king adjoined the palace. Today the *Place Dauphine* and the *Pont Neuf* are at that location. P. Paulin'" (*Berte*, 176).

lines 313, 584, 948, 3188: Saint Richier's (Riquier's) activity in northern France may bring him easily to the narrator's mind. Born at Celles near Amiens, he received training as a priest from Irish missionaries whom he had protected from inhabitants of the area while still a young man and a pagan. After becoming a priest, he spent several years in England before returning to Celles and founding a monastery there. A renowned preacher, he issued warnings to King Dagobert and other powerful people. He later lived as a hermit at Forest-Moûtier, where he died 26 April, 645. His relics were eventually moved to the town in Somme that bears his name, and a monastery was founded there. Alcuin (d. 803) rewrote a life of Saint Riquier, as did Hariwulf, a twelfth-century abbot of Oudenbourg near Bruges.[8]

line 369: This line reads in Old French, "On doit bien reculer por le plus long saillir." Hassell identifies the idea in this line as proverbial. He cites nearly a column of its occurrences in Middle French literature.[9] The reference in *Berte* shows that of course this proverb did not originate with the fourteenth century.

---

[6] Charles G. Herbermann, et. al. eds., *The Catholic Encyclopedia*, (New York: The Encyclopedia Press, Inc., 1913), 11:251.

[7] David Hugh Farmer, *The Oxford Dictionary of Saints* (Oxford: Oxford University Press, 1978), 83.

[8] René Aigrain, *L'hagiographie: Ses sources, ses méthodes, son histoire*, Subsidia Hagiographica 80 (Brussels: Société des Bollandistes, 2000), 164, 311.

[9] J.W. Hassell, Jr., *Middle French Proverbs, Sentences, and Proverbial Phrases* (Toronto: Pontifical Institute of Mediaeval Studies, 1982), 214 (no. R15).

line 664: Saint Simon, not to be confused with Simon Peter, was one of the apostles. Tradition says that he preached in Egypt and Persia along with Saint Jude, with whom he was martyred. (*The Lives of Saints*, 441).

lines 700–1168: Comparing specific phrases in *Berte* with those in *chansons de geste* describing the battlefield anguish of male protagonists, Yasmina Foehr-Janssens, in her article "Une Reine au désert: désolation et majesté dans *Berte as grans piés* d'Adenet le Roi," shows that Adenet lends an atmosphere of epic grandeur to Bertha's ordeal in the forest. Foehr-Janssen points out that these echoes of classic *chansons de geste* also add to a sense of Bertha's personal majesty, as does her intense piety during these scenes. Foehr-Janssens notes that Adenet insists upon Bertha's refinement and purity throughout his narrative, in contrast to other versions. All of these elements contribute, Foehr-Janssens points out, to the dignity and nobility of Bertha as Charlemagne's mother and in turn to the magnificence of the emperor's own legend.[10]

lines 731, 974, 984: In need of shelter, Bertha invokes Saint Julien, patron saint of travelers. The legend of Saint Julien tells that he returned from hunting to discover what he thought was his wife in bed with another man. Enraged, he killed the couple, who turned out to be his own visiting mother and father, whom his wife had had sleep in Julien's and her bed. In penance for his deed, Julien founded a hospital for the poor and spent his life ferrying travelers across a river. Although stained-glass church windows and paintings depict his story, no basis for it in fact exists (*Oxford Dictionary of Saints*, 226–227). In the nineteenth century Gustave Flaubert retold the story as one of his *Trois Contes*.

lines 890–893: According to legend unsupported by fact, the martyr Saint Barbara gave protection from lightning, which is mentioned in line 839 of *Berte*. Barbara's father, who persecuted her for her Christian faith, was killed by lightning (*Oxford Dictionary of Saints*, 28).

lines 891–893: The story of Saint Katherine (Catherine of Alexandria), apparently invented, began in the ninth century and was brought back to Europe by crusaders. She was very popular in the Middle Ages. Considering herself the bride of Christ, she refused marriage with the emperor Maxentius (third century). In addition, she successfully defended Christianity in arguments with philosophers. She was tortured on a wheel, which broke, and was then decapitated.

---

[10] Yasmina Foehr-Janssens, "Une Reine au désert: désolation et majesté dans *Berte as grans piés* d'Adenet le Roi," in *L'Épopée romane au Moyen Age et aux temps modernes: Actes du XIV Congrès International de la Société Rencesvals pour l'étude des Épopées Romanes (Naples, 24–30 juillet 1997)*, ed. S. Luongo, 2 vols. (Naples: Fredericiana Editrice Universitaria, 2001), 229–45, here 230, 234–39, 244–45.

Venerated by several groups, her celebrated chastity made her the patron saint of virgins and young girls. She is no longer officially recognized (*Oxford Dictionary of Saints*, 69-70).

lines 1083–1147: Like the famously tempted Saint Anthony, the desert fathers of the third and fourth centuries believed that obliterating the passions and the appetites could prepare one for direct knowledge of God.[11] They therefore tried to eat as little as possible, and to avoid thoughts of sex and certainly the company of women, who might arouse their passions and remain in their memories. From time to time, demons appeared to them disguised as beautiful women, whom it was necessary to resist. The *Historia Monachorum in Aegypto* relates the journey of a group of travelers in 304-5 A.D. who visited several hermits in Egypt to whom these ideas were important. Among the warnings related to sex encountered on these visits is a story reminiscent of Bertha's in its initial stages. The hermit John of Lycopolis tells of a holy man who is visited by a beautiful woman in great distress. Lost in the desert and overtaken by night, she begs for shelter. Unlike Adenet's hermit, the man takes pity upon her and invites her in. Having at length aroused the man's passions, the woman—actually a demon—vanishes (*The Lives of the Desert Fathers*, 57).

lines 1169–1421: A late fourteenth- to early fifteenth-century collection of medieval French tales translated into Castilian served as a companion to pilgrims on the road to Saint James of Compostela. The stories prominently feature exiled and falsely accused women and also deal with the relationship between guest and host. The codex has recently been published as *Libro de los huéspedes* (*Escorial MS H. I. B.*): *A Critical Edition* by John K. Moore, Jr.

lines 1223, 2019, 2269: Saint Vincent may refer to Saint Vincent of Saragossa, a Spanish martyr who is known to have died during the reign of Diocletian in 304 A.D. He was born in Saragossa and received his education there from Bishop Valerius. Numerous churches were built in his honor in Spain, France, and Italy (*Catholic Encyclopedia*, 15: 434).

lines 1262, 1774: Saint Germain's name works here as an end rhyme, but it may be significant that Constance invokes him when she agrees to care for Bertha when Symon brings her in cold, hungry, and exhausted from her ordeal in the forest. Saint Germain, or Germanus, born in the Autun area about 496, became bishop of Paris. He was notable for his care of the poor. The Paris church Saint-Germain-des-Prés is named in his honor. A church on that site was built by King Childebert, who was greatly influenced by Germain and had become Christian. That church was dedicated to Saint Vincent because of an incident Childebert

---

[11] *The Lives of the Desert Fathers* (*The Historia Monachorum in Aegypto*), trans. Russell Norman (Oxford and Kalamazoo: Mowbray and Cistercian Publications, 1981), 126.

had experienced in Saragossa. Childebert had been about to sack Saragossa, but, touched by the residents' appeal to the protection of Saint Vincent of Saragossa, did not. The bishop then gave Childebert the martyr's stole. Childebert built the church in Paris to house the relic (*Catholic Encyclopedia*, 6: 473).

lines 1278, 1783: Latin translations of works that were supposedly derived from texts of writers who witnessed the Trojan War were available in medieval Europe and were used as sources for Benoît de Sainte-Maure's *Roman de Troie* (between 1155 and 1160).[12] Thus information about Helen was available in Adenet's time from all these materials, and her name was an easy metaphor for feminine beauty. Matthew Gumpert cites, for example, a thirteenth-century French poem of "amour de loin" (love from afar) in which the poet, Raoul de Soissons, names Helen ("Elaine") as a paragon of beauty, as does Adenet in these lines (101).

line 1345: "De mauvaise marrastre est l'amor molt petite" reads this line, reinforcing the proverbial citations from the fourteenth and fifteenth centuries given by Hassell (*Proverbs*, 160, no. M81) for "Pire que marâtre" ("worse than a stepmother").

lines 1383–1417: Other women in thirteenth-century French literature who are away from home and family make their living by needlework. In *L'Escoufle*, written by Jean Renart between 1200 and 1202, Aélis, separated from her lover Guillaume with whom she has eloped, shelters with a mother and daughter who earn their living making *guimpes* (wimples for nuns). Isabelle, the daughter, goes with Aélis to Montpellier where Isabelle makes *guimpes* and Aélis does fine needlework with gold and silk thread, supporting themselves thereby. Similarly, Frêne, in *Galeran de Bretagne*, also written at the turn of the twelfth and thirteenth centuries and by Jean Renart according to some scholars, is forced from the convent that was her home and takes refuge with a mother and daughter of Rouen, where she earns money by needlework and teaches the daughter to work with silk and gold thread.

line 1395: Saint Nicholas was a Greek bishop of Myra, now in modern-day Turkey. Few facts have been established about his life, but his legend associates him with gift-giving. Said to have provided dowries for three poor young women, he is the patron saint of unmarried girls and children, which may explain his invocation here by Constance's daughter (*Oxford Dictionary of Saints*, 292).

line 1432: The legend of Longinus identifies him as the Roman soldier at the crucifixion who pierced Christ's side with a lance and declared that Christ was truly

---

[12] Matthew Gumpert, *Grafting Helen: The Abduction of the Classical Past* (Madison: University of Wisconsin Press, 2001), 130–31.

the Son of God. Stories have him healed of poor eyesight by Christ's blood and later persecuted for his faith (*Oxford Dictionary of Saints*, 248).

lines 1507–1520: "References to the 'Saxon matter' (compare, for example, *la Chanson des Saines* of Jehan Bodel), Adenet having imagined himself, it seems, in addition, the entanglements of Justamont with Floire's granddaughter" (*Berte*, 178).

lines 1530, 1763: The woodcutting and logs referred to in these lines could be references to a thirteenth-century practice Georges Duby mentions: sometimes landowners had their foresters allow workers to sell wood in small lots, augmenting the workers' income.[13]

lines 1557–1559: Reading "Dieus consent mainte gent traïson a fournir, / Mais en la fin le set Dieus si a point merir / Que leur traÿson pert ains qu'il puissent morir," these lines recall the proverb Hassell lists (*Proverbs*, 240 no. T77), citing fifteenth-century sources: "Trahison retourne à son maistre" (Betrayal returns to its master). Line 2300 is similar: "Qui traÿson pourchace, drois est qu'il s'en repente." Adenet expresses in both instances a more complicated idea than is in the proverb.

line 1560: "Car Dieus fait maintes fois droit à droit revenir" is the proverb Hassell records (*Proverbs*, 98, no. D126), giving fourteenth- and fifteenth-century occurrences, as "Droit à droit revient" ("Right comes back to right").

line 1665: "Que traÿson et murdre couvient k'en la fin paire" restates the proverb "Meurtre ne se peut celer" ("Murder cannot hide"), which Hassell cites (*Proverbs*, 165, no. M148), quoting a fifteenth-century source.

lines 1692, 2129, 2598, 2871, 3138: On 24 December, 496, Saint Remi (Remigius) baptized Clovis, king of the Franks. Remi, son of a prominent family of Picardy—his father was the count of Laon—became bishop of Reims at the age of twenty-two after distinguishing himself at the school there. Before his conversion, Clovis had already expressed his admiration for Remi through generous gifts to him and the cathedral at Reims. Afterward, he granted large tracts of land to Remi, who established bishoprics in Tournai, Cambrai, Thérouanne, Arras and Laon. Remi was noted for his influence on colleagues and others. Sidonius Apollinarus thought highly of his sermons. A few of his writings remain extant (*Catholic Encyclopedia*, 12: 763-764). Saint Remi's important association with northern France and southern Flanders, territories familiar to Adenet, may account for the frequent mention of him.

---

[13] Georges Duby, *Rural Economy and Country Life in the Medieval West*, trans. Cynthia Postan (Columbia, SC: University of South Carolina Press, 1968), 145.

line 1831: Among the many calumnies Jews endured in the Middle Ages was that of poisoning the water wells. In the Black Death of the fourteenth century, Jews were widely accused of causing the disease by poisoning the wells.[14]

line 1990: The street in question is " the present-day *rue Saint-Denis*" (*Berte*, 178).

line 2060: The Saint Marcel referred to here may be Saint Marcellus, a centurion executed in 298 A.D. for refusing to participate in what he regarded as the impious celebration of the emperor of Rome's birthday, instead declaring himself a Christian.[15]

line 2229: The legend of the Antichrist arose in connection with traditions of apocalyptic eschatology, or divine revelations of end times, which grew out of ancient Jewish experiences of control and persecution by foreign powers. Apocalyptic texts, of which some of the earliest are Enoch I and the Book of Daniel, view history as under God's control. The pattern of events presents a crisis in which an evil and deceitful person (called the Antichrist in the New Testament) inflicts great persecution and destruction. People who participate in evil are part of a collective Antichrist. The crisis precedes God's judgment, in which the wicked are punished, the Antichrist defeated, and the just vindicated and rewarded. This pattern recurs throughout history with minor figures leading up in end times to the final cataclysm and the ultimate Antichrist. A tenth-century description of the Antichrist by the monk Adso set the standard ideas for the Antichrist for several centuries.[16]

line 2309: "As in line 2239, *main thoroughfare* here designates the present-day *rue Saint-Martin*, which led to Montfaucon, where the gallows was" (*Berte*, 178).

line 2535: Saint Amant, also known as Saint Amand, was a friend of Jonas de Bobbio, and an important seventh-century missionary to Central Europe, associated with Maestricht. Jonas wrote a biography of Saint Vaast, a bishop of Arras who died in 540. Saint Amand died a little after 675 at Elnone, his monastery. He life was written around the turn of the eighth century and was added to by Milon d'Elnone, who died in 871 or 872 (Aigrain, *L'hagiographie,* 163–65).

line 2593: The *quintain* in line 2596 refers to the target at which the practicing jouster would tilt; in line 2044 the *quintain* is the sport of such tilting.

---

[14] Avner Falk, *Anti-Semitism: A History and Psychoanalysis of Contemporary Hatred* (Westport, CT and London: Praeger Publishers, 2008), 34.

[15] The Benedictine Monks of Saint Augustine's Abbey, Ramsgate, *The Book of Saints* (London: A&C Black, 1989), 567.

[16] Bernard McGinn, *Antichrist: Two Thousand Years of the Human Fascination with Evil* (San Francisco: HarperSanFrancisco, 1994), 2–15, 54, 79, 144.

line 2843: Numerous interesting details are known about the life of Saint Eloi (Eligius). Born of Gallo-Roman parents about 590 near Limoges, he worked under a well-known goldsmith, Abbo, master of the mint at Limoges. Later in Neustria, Eloi was commissioned to construct a golden throne encrusted with gems for Clotaire II, who thought so highly of his character and skill that he made him part of his household and appointed him master of the mint at Marseilles. Upon Clotaire's death, Eloi became chief councilor to his son, Dagobert I. Eloi persuaded the Breton king to submit to Dagobert's authority. Through his influence with the king, Eloi secured alms for the poor and freedom for captives arriving each day at Marseilles from many lands. He built churches and monasteries, became bishop of Noyon-Tournai, and spent many years converting people throughout the Flanders/Belgium region. He died 1 December 660, at Noyon. Eloi is the patron saint of goldsmiths and other metal workers and of blacksmiths (*Catholic Encyclopedia*, vol. 5, 386). Eloi would have been well known in regions familiar to Adenet. The saint's reputation for honesty may account for his invocation at this point.

lines 3226–3227: *Label, gules,* and *besant* are terms of heraldry. The *label* was a small bar from which hung pendants, three usually; it distinguished the younger son from the elder during the father's lifetime. *Gules* means the color red. A *bezant* was a coin-shaped gold object called *bezant* after a gold coin from Byzantium or Constantinople used in Europe for centuries.

lines 3398–3399: These lines, "Pour ce fait bon bien faire, chascuns i doit penser, / K'en la fin pert li biens, tant ne peut demorer," bring to mind the proverb which Hassell, with fourteenth- and fifteenth-century sources, states (*Proverbs,* 56, no. B142) as "Une bonté (ung bien) requiert l'autre." In English the saying goes, "One good deed deserves another." Once again Adenet's idea is more complex than that of the proverb.

In his "Table of Proper Names" for *Berte as grans piés*, Henry informs us that Strigon in line 119 refers to the "town of Esztergom or Gran, in Hungary at the confluence of the Hron and the Danube" (198). He identifies a town named Octrente (line 274) in the Old French as Otranto (197), an important seaport in southern Italy. The Betee Sea of line 480 lies beyond the Betis mountain range in southern Spain. Henry identifies Lutise of line 804 as "the country of Leutices, a pagan people" (196). Henry tells us that the tower of Argoise referred to in line 1525 is in Poland (193) and that Delfur (line 1003) was a Chaldean city (195). Henry believes that Adenet made up the name Valberte in line 3453 (*Berte aus grans piés,* 257).